Computer Programming For Beginners

Learn The Fundamentals Of Computer Programming Languages

+

JAVASCRIPT

Learn the Fundamentals of the JavaScript Computer Programming Language

By: Marc Rawen

Introduction

Since you have bought this book, I must say, 'Welcome to the wonderful world of programming!' You see, programming is not just an activity but an entire world on its and by learning a language, you will be taking your first steps into this brave new world. After all, computers and computing technologies are everywhere, and a programming language is a foundation on which all of them are made possible.

Now, you may be interested in learning a programming language for a career in one of the many tech careers or simply as a hobby. Whatever be your reason, the fact is that you need to choose the right programming language to start with. You should learn some of the easiest programming languages to build up a strong base before proceeding further.

As such, this book deals with some of the best programming languages that a beginner should learn first before moving on to the harder ones. In this book, you will be learning the basics of Java, C, C++, Python, JavaScript and Ruby. You will certainly be discovering the specialties of this language and the areas they excel in. At the same time, you will be getting a comprehensive introduction to them so that you can jump in and start learning the language.

Before proceeding, you should remember that programming, even in the easy languages, can be difficult for the beginner. As such, you need to be patient and be ready to put in some effort so that you can succeed. As you learn, you will start finding it easier and finally make your own unique programs.

Let's us now start on the journey of programming.

Chapter 1: An Introduction To Programming

Before you start learning a particular language, you should have a proper understanding of programming. The absolute basics of programming are a must. It will help you in understanding the fundamentals of any language better.

Binary Numbers

Computers and nearly all computer based devices use the binary numeral system in their functioning. This system comprises of only two numbers, 1 and 0. Each of them is referred to as a bit. All computer programs can be simplified down to this system. In fact, the binary system has a key role in how computers store information and data of all kinds.

At the fundamental level, computers simply switch from 1 to 0 for all of their functions, no matter how simple or complex. Any data, including text and images, are stored in the computer in the form of a series of 1s and 0s. You see, computers are electrical circuits. In a circuit, an electrical current either flows in a specific line or it does. Therefore, the state can be defined as either a 1 or a 0. In other words, it is a binary situation.

Once you understand this concept, you will realize why the binary system is such basic computers. In all computers programs and situations, a problem can always be simplified down to a binary choice. As such, all computers process information using the binary system.

What is a Program?

Let us first analyze the function of a computer. Its primary function is to solve a problem. Now, how does it solve it? It does so with the help of a program. Computer programs are sequences of instructions which perform a specific task when they are executed by the computer.

No matter what the computer is, it will remain completely useless it has the right set of programs. If you are reading this book on a computer-based device, it is only because the device has a program that allows it do so.

What is a Programming Language?

As the name suggests, a programming language is a specialized language that is used for programming.

Now, there is a native programming language that all computers have and understand. This is referred to as machine code. Unfortunately, machine code can be extremely difficult for people to understand. Among other things, machine code is nearly always expressed in the binary system. Moreover, the machine code is unique to specific computer architecture. As a result, it is possible for two computers to use two variants of machine code.

Therefore, you need some way to communicate with the computers. This is why other programming languages exist. They act as an interface between people and the computer. With them, programs can be expressed in languages which can be understood by people easily. At the same time, the language will be common to different computer architectures. More importantly, the programs can be translated to machine code easily.

To make sure that this happens, a computer has to interpret or compile the program written in a programming language so that the program is executed. You need to understand compilation and interpretation with respect to computer programming.

For a compiled program, a complier has to be used so that the program can be translated into machine code for the computer to use. However, the source code will not be run by the computer in the case of an interpreted program. Instead, an interpreter reads each line of the program as it is running and modifies it into the machine code. Once modified, the computer executes that line of the program.

Programming languages can use either one of these approaches or both. Each of them has its own advantages when it comes to programming and software development. Generally, compiled programs can take longer to develop, but they can run faster. After all, the computer will execute a program that has already been translated. Interpreted programs take longer to run as they need to be translated every time they are executed. However, they can be written faster as the languages are generally simpler. At the same time, the entire program will not to be compiled after every modification or bug test.

Tips for Programming

When you are programming, you will be learning a lot of new things. As such, things can get confusing very quickly unless you can keep a track. In many cases, learners even forget a few basic principles about programming. Remember these details to ensure that you don't feel that you are getting in way over your head.

- When you are trying to develop a program, you should ensure that it can fulfill the need for which it is being created in the first place.

- You should also make sure that your program can be easily used by other people.

- You must be ready to invest a significant amount of time while learning programming.

- On the other hand, you need to make sure that your program can be understood, improved and fixed in a short period of time.

• Before starting a program, check out the other programs that are similar to what you want to create. Understand those programs and find out what their strong and weak points are. You should think of ways through which the program can be improved.

• You need to plan what you want your program to be capable of before you start writing it. You can create a flowchart of the functions and features of the program beforehand.

• If possible, try to discover some good source code for programs that are similar to yours. Make sure of the quality of the code.

• When writing a program, you need to maximize the functionality while decreasing the complexity. This is the way you create a truly effective program.

• You should develop your program in such a way that it is possible to understand what is happening by simply taking a look at the source code.

• You should add comments whenever you are attempting the complicated of the program. This can be helpful for you in the long run.

• When defining variables, you must always use names that are easily understood and simple. This helps you to keep track of them and the functions that they will be used in.

You should now have an idea of what programming is like. Now, it is time to select which programming language you should try out.

Chapter 2: Go Old School With C And C++

Both C and C++ have a rich history as programming languages. C was developed in the early 1970s, and it has gone from strength to strength while C++ came about later in the 1980s.

You need to remember that both of these languages have been present in the early days of computer programming. As such, they are considered among the most foundational programming languages in the world. Therefore, you are sure to benefit greatly by learning them even if you do not use them later. In fact, learning them is like gaining an invaluable insight into the very beginnings of computer programming.

There are advantages and disadvantages to each language certainly. Nonetheless, you will gain a better understanding of programming in general. In fact, you may even find it easier to start learning other programming languages such as Java. After all, the features of C and C++ have served as an inspiration for quite a few languages.

Of course, there is a question of choice between C and C++. Now, C is the older of the two and C++ is considered to be a subset of the earlier language. C++ is also considered to be the easier of the two by many programmers. On the other hand, knowledge of C can prove to be helpful if you are hoping to become a professional programmer. Nonetheless, it is quite possible to learn C after learning C++ and vice versa.

The Design of C

C is a procedural programming language, and it was designed so as to be compiled with a relatively straightforward compiler. Its design also provides language constructs that can be mapped efficiently to machine instructions. The runtime support required is also minimal. These features enabled C to become useful for a variety of applications which had to be coded with assembly language previously.

In spite of the low-level capabilities of C, this programming language was meant to encourage programming on a cross-platform level. It is possible to compile a C program for a range of operating systems and computer platforms along as it is portably written and is standards-compliant.

A Simple Program in C

In order to illustrate the programming language of C, it helps if you have an example to look at. Here is a simple 'Hello World' program written in this language.

#include <stdio.h>

```
intmain ()

{

Printf ("Hello world\n");

Return o;

}
```

To better understand what is happening in the program, it helps to break it up into different sections and tackle them one by one.

#include<stdio.h>

This code tells the program to include a file named 'stdio.h'which stands for Standard Input/ Output header file. With it, it is possible to use specific commands for input or output in the program. In this example, it allows us to output a message and print it on the screen.

Intmain ()

The int is known as the return value, and it is of the type integer in this example. The next part is the main () which is the main function. Every program in C has to have only one main function, and it is also the starting point for all programs.

Printf ("Hello World\n");

The printf command is used when things need to be printed on the screen which is 'Hello World' in this program. The data which is going to be printed have to place inside round brackets. In this case, 'Hello World' is placed inside inverted commas as it is a string and strings have to be placed inside inverted commas. The last part of the command is \n and it is known as an escape sequence. The \n symbolizes a newline character, and it allows the next output to be printed on the next line. There are other kinds of escape sequences which you will learn during C programming.

Return o;

In the second line of the program, 'intmain ()' was written to denote that the main function has to return an integer. By using the 'return o' command, the value null will be returned to the operating system. By returning a zero, you are simply telling the OS that no errors occurred when running the program.

Based on this example, there are a few things you should know about programming in this language.

- All programs written should have a single main function.

- The execution of the program will always start from the main function.

- The execution of the program will always start at the opening brace of the function and stop at the closing brace. Braces can be used to group together statements.

- Typically, all statements are written in lowercase letters in C.

- Uppercase letters are reserved for messages, output strings, and symbolic names

- You must declare a variable with the right data type before using it.

- All statements in C have to end with a semicolon.

Data Types in C

In C, you will find a standard set of fundamental data types. Due to their simplicity, they are often referred to as primitive data types. However, it is possible to develop a range of complex data structures from them. There are a total of four basic data types:

- Character - char

- Integer - int

- Floating-point - float

- double floating-point - double

The actual range and size of the data types may vary among compiles and processor types. It is possible to modify the behavior of the variable type to which they are applied with the help of data type qualifiers. There are a few qualifiers in C.

Size qualifiers can change the size of the data type. Two size qualifiers are present in C. They are 'short' and 'long'. They simply change the size of the declared variable.

Sign qualifiers determine what kind of numbers that the variable can hold. The 'signed' qualifier denotes that the variable can contain positive as well as negative numbers. However, an 'unsigned' variable can only contain positive numbers. It is not necessary to declare a variable assigned as variables are signed by default. These qualifiers can be applied to the char and int data types.

The constant qualifier is used to declare that the value of an identifier will remain unchanged in the program. In other words, its value is constant. The keyword for this qualifier is 'const'. If you want the value of a variable to be changed by external sources, you can declare it to be 'volatile'. This is another variable that you should become familiar with.

Variables

As you may know, variables are a specific location in the memory where data is stored by a program. The size of the memory block depends on the type of the variable. For identifying the memory block, you need to assign a unique name to each variable. Before variables can be used, they need to be declared with their data type and name. The syntax for variable declaration in C is given below.

[Storage-class] type data variable name [= initial value];

You do not have to define the initial value or the storage class for the variable if they are not required. It is possible to declare multiple variables at the same time as long as you want them to have the same storage class and data type. The syntax to do so is given below.

[Storage-class] type data variable name [= initial value] variable [= initial value];

Statements

In C, statements allow you to control the flow of the execution of your program. The C programming language offers you a variety of statements. Some of the most commonly used statements are given below.

- If statement
- goto statement
- switch statement
- while statement
- do-while statement
- For statement

As you proceed with programming in C, you will come across many other concepts such as input and output functions, arrays, structure, pointers and so on. Once you know about them, you can easily jump into other programming languages such as C++ and Java.

When you are writing software or applications, you will need to use Loops. This is an essential technique prevalent in all programming languages. A loop can be defined as a sequence of instructions which are repeated continually till a certain predefined condition is met. In simple terms, a block of code is repeated a set number of times till a condition are fulfilled.

Generally in a loop, a certain process is performed. This can be as simple as fetching a specific data item and modifying it. After it, a condition is checked. For example, a counter can be checked to see if it has reached a specific number. If the number has not been reached, the next instruction for the program is to return to the very first instruction of the sequence. As such, the sequence is repeated. Once the condition has been fulfilled, the instruction will cause the program to proceed to the next set of sequential instructions. It can also branch out from the loop.

There is a special kind of loop known as an infinite loop. In this loop, there is an absence of a functioning exit instruction. As a result, the loop will repeat continually till it is sensed by the operating system which will terminate the program and an error will show. The infinite loop can also be stopped due to the occurrence of some other event. For example, the program can be made to terminate automatically after a specific duration of time.

In C#, you will come across four different kinds of loops. As such, you need to be familiar with them.

The while Loop

The simplest of the four loops in C# is the while loop. In this type of loop, a sequence of instructions will be executed continually as long as the defined condition returns true. It will only exit when the condition returns false. Here is an example to help you understand it.

```
using System;


namespace ConsoleApplication1
{
    class Program
    {
        static void Main(string[] args)
        {
            Int number = 0;


            while (number < 10)
            {
                Console.WriteLine (number);
                number = number + 1;
            }
```

```
        Console.ReadLine ();

      }

    }

  }
```

When you run this code, you will find that the program lists a sequence of numbers in the console starting at 0 and ending at 10.

Of course, the variable number is first defined as 0. Every time that the loop is executed, the variable is incremented by 1. You can see this happening in this statement:

number = number + 1

As a result, the program keeps displaying the numbers till it reaches nine which is the last thing to be displayed. You may be wondering why nine is being displayed when you have mentioned 10 in the code.

The condition will only be true when the number is less than 10. Once the number becomes 10, the condition becomes false. After all, ten is not less than 10. As you can see, the condition of the while loop is checked before the program enters the loop sequence. Once the number turns 10, the condition becomes false, and the while loop sequence is not executed.

The do Loop

The do loop shares certain similarities with the while loop with one major difference. The while loop checks the condition before the loop sequence is executed. On the other hand, the do loop will check the condition after the loop has been executed. This means the loop sequence will always be executed at least one time before exiting. This is not possible with the while loop. Take a look at the following example.

using System;

namespace ConsoleApplication1

{

  class Program

  {

    static void Main(string[] args)

    {

      Int number = 0;

```
        do
        {
            Console.WriteLine (number);
            number = number + 1;
        } while (number < 10)


            Console.ReadLine ();
        }
    }
}
```

On running this program, you will see the numbers being displayed from 0 to 9. Once the number becomes 10 or more than 10, the program will exit the loop sequence. As you can see, the do loop functions in a similar manner to the while loop but checks the condition after the execution of a sequence.

The for Loop

The for loop is different from that of the do or the while loops. The for loop is generally used when you know the exact number of iterations that you want. It can also be used when you have defined a variable that contains the amount. The following example illustrates the use of the for loop.

```
using System;


namespace ConsoleApplication1
{
    class Program
    {
        static void Main(string[] args)
        {
            Int number = 10;


            for (Int i = 0; i < number; i++)
```

```
        Console.WriteLine (i);


    Console.ReadLine ();
  }
 }
}
```

When you run this program, you will find that the output is the same as that of the previous examples. However, the for loop tends to be more compact than the while, and the do loops, as you can see.

There are three parts to the for loop. First, a variable is initialized for counting. Then, a conditional statement is defined to test the variable. Finally, we increment the counter variable. In C# and a few other programming languages, you can use ++ instead of writing the entire statement: "variable = variable + 1" The result will be the same.

The first section will be executed only once before the actual loop starts. This is the section where the variable i is defined and then set to 0. The next two sections will be executed for each iteration of the for loop. In each repetition, the variable I will be compared to the number variable. When the variable i is less than the number variable, the loop will run once again. After the execution, the variable I will be increased by 1. In this case, it will continue to loop till variable I become equal to 10.

The for each Loop

The for each loop is quite different from the previous three loops. This loop operates on a collection of items. Arrays or other kinds of built-in list types can also be used. For the following example, an ArrayList is used as it is one of the simple lists available in C#. ArrayList tends to work in a similar to an array.

```
using System;

Using System.Collections;


namespace ConsoleApplication1
{
    class Program
    {
        static void Main(string[] args)
        {
            ArrayList list = new ArrayList ();
```

```
        list.Add ("Dog");
        list.Add ("Cat");
        list.Add ("Bird");

        foreach (string name in list)
            Console.WriteLine (name);

        Console.ReadLine ();
    }
  }
}
```

As you can see, an instance of an ArrayList is created first in the code. This is followed by the addition of a few string items to the list. In this example, we have added a few names of animals as string items to the ArrayList list.

The foreach loop is then used to run through each of the items. In each repetition, the name variable is set to the item that has been reached in the ArrayList. This variable is then pushed for output. As a result, you can see the animals that were inserted into the ArrayList being displayed on the console

It is vital that you inform the foreach loop as to which data type you are looking to take out of the collection. In this case, we have specified that the name variable will belong to the string data type. It is possible that you have a list of different data types. In such cases, you can use the object class rather than a specific class so as to take out each item of the list as an object.

If you are going to be using collections in your programs, you will find the foreach loop to be the best choice among all the loop types available in C#. This is mainly because the foreach is simpler than all of the other loops when it comes to such operations.

Chapter 3: Enjoy The Versatility Of Java

Java is one of the most influential programming languages in the world. It also remained popular and pervasive in the computing world. You can discover Java being used on all kinds of platforms, from the web to operating systems and even devices. You will find Java to be filled with features. As a programming language, it is class based and object oriented. It has been designed to be portable so that you can work on it on a wide variety of platforms. This is why it is still popular all over the world even two decades after its initial release.

On the other hand, Java can be difficult to understand at times and hard to program efficiently and effectively. However, its popularity means that you will not lack for resources to help you understand or avenues to explore as a programmer. Another benefit of learning Java is that it forces you to think analytically and logically. In other words, you will start thinking like a programmer. You can get a better understanding of how computers process information as well. The core concepts and fundamentals that you learn in Java will prove to be useful when you start learning other programming languages.

The Features of Java

Java was originally developed in 1991 by Sun Microsystems Inc. Now, it is maintained by Oracle Corporation who acquired Sun Microsystems in 2009. Its popularity hinges on its excellent features.

- **Platform Independence:** Unlike some other programming languages, Java is platform independent. As a result, you can run Java programs on all platforms no matter which platform you compiled them on.

- **Object Oriented:** While Java is an object oriented programming language, it lacks some complex features such as multiple inheritances, operator overloading, and explicit memory allocation. As a result, it is a simple language to learn.

- **Strong Language:** Mishandled runtime errors and memory management are two of the main issues that result in program failures. In Java, these issues can be efficiently taken care of. Exception handling procedures can resolve mishandled runtime errors while garbage collection can take care of memory management mistakes.

- **Security:** When writing Java programs, all codes will remain confined inside the Java Runtime Environment. As a result, unauthorized access to the system resources is not granted.

- **Multithreading:** Due to its support for multithreading, Java allows your program to perform different tasks at the same time.

A Simple Program in Java

To gain a better understanding of what Java is like, the following example will be of help. This is a Hello World program, a simple program that is often used for illustrating the basics of a programming language. You will already have come across such an example in the chapter on C and C++.

```
Public class Main {
Public static void main (String [] args) {
System.out.println ("Hello, World!");
    }
}
```

Now, let us examining each section of the program to understand what the functions and keywords are and what they do.

Public class Main {

This is the first line of the program, and it defines a class called Main. If you want a line of code to run in a Java program, you have to place it inside a class. Here the class Main is declared. It has been defined as public. Therefore, other classes can access it. You should also remember that a public class must be declared inside a file which has the same name. In this case, the name of the file should be Main.java. If you do not do so, you will get an error during compilation.

Public static void main (String [] args) {

This is the starting point of the Java program. It is necessary for the main method to have the exact signature shown so that the program can be run. Here are a few of the keywords that you need to take a look into. You are already familiar with public, and the others will be discussed shortly. 'Main' is, of course, the name of the method.

System.out.println ("Hello, World!");

The system is a predefined class in Java, and it contains some variables and methods which are useful while programming. The next keyword is out, and it is a static variable from System. It is representative of the program output. PrintIn is a method found inside out and it is used for printing a line.

Datatypes and Variables in Java

In Java, there are three kinds of variables and several data types. Understanding them is vital when you want to write programs in this language.

Data Types

There are two kinds of data types in Java, primitive and non-primitive. Primitive data types are predefined and provided by Java. Some examples of these in Java include Boolean, char, int, long, short and float. On the other hand, non-primitive data types are not defined by Java. Instead, they will be created by you, the programmer. They refer to a memory location which is why they are sometimes known as reference variables. String and array are some of the non-primitive data types.

Variables

In Java, there are three kinds of variables that you can use for your programs. The type depends on how you declare the variable. Local variables are those which are declared inside a method. On the other hand, instance variables are defined outside the method but inside the class. Static variables are simply those variables that are declared with the static keyword, and they cannot be local variables. You will learn about these uses when you start programming in Java in earnest.

As with other programming languages, you need to declare a variable before it can be used. The basic syntax for declaring a variable in Java is given below.

Data type variable [= value];

You can declare multiple variables of the samedatatype in a single statement. You just need to use a comma to separate them.

In Java, you need to take care when you are declaring variables as there are rules in place for it. The names for variables are case-sensitive. Therefore, 'Hi' and 'hi' will be considered as two separate variables. In fact, it is a good practice to avoid starting variable names with capitals as such a format is usually applied to class names. You can use the '$' and '_' signs but use them intelligently. Whitespace is not allowed in variable names, and you cannot start a name with a number. Finally, you cannot use a reserved word or keyword as a variable name.

Loops and Conditional Statements

In a program, statements and lines of codes are executed in a sequential manner. However, it is possible to create complex execution paths to make certain programs and functions possible. This is achieved by means of different control structures such as conditional statements and loops.

Loops

A loop statement is used when a block of code needs to be executed multiple times. There are different kinds of loop statements available in Java for specific situations. They are listed as follows.

- **While loop:** This will cause a group of statements to be repeated as long as a given condition remains true. Once the condition becomes false, the loop will no longer be executed. The condition will be tested before the loop is executed.

- **Do-While loop:** This loop works in a similar manner to the while loop. However, it will check the condition after the code in the loop has been executed.

- **For loop:** Here, a block of code will be executed a set number of times. It allows the code which manages the variable for the loop to be shortened.

Conditional Statements

These are actually structures that are accompanied by one or multiple conditions. Those conditions are evaluated by the program and the statements executed according to the result of the evaluation. If the condition is true, a specific statement or set of statements will be executed. If false, another set of statements will be executed. In other words, these structures allow the program to make decisions. Java offers a few kinds of conditional structures to be used.

- **If statement:** This contains a Boolean expression along with the statements that are to be executed when the condition is true.

- **If else statement:** This is a regular if statement used alongside an else statement. If the condition is false, the statements listed under the else statement will be executed. The code under the if statement is executed when it returns true.

- **Nested if statements:** This is a special use of the if statement. It is possible to nest if statements inside one another. It is also applicable for if else statements.

- **Switch statement:** This statement used to test a variable for equality against a specified list of values. Each value will have a statement or block of code that will be executed when the value of the variable matches it.

These are some of the basics that you should be familiar with when you are learning how to develop programs using the Java language. As mentioned earlier, Java is an excellent stepping stone to the world of programming. Once learned, you will find it easier to learn other languages.

Advantages Offered by JavaScript

JavaScript offers a range of benefits to the users. Some of them are given below.

Simplicity: JavaScript, like HTML and CSS, is quite easy to learn. Moreover, you can also start implementing JavaScript code with equal ease.

Speed: JavaScript is executed on the client-side. As a result, all code functions can be executed immediately. There is no need to contact the server and then wait for a response. This allows JavaScript to be quite fast.

Versatility: JavaScript is compatibility with quite a few other languages. It is, in fact, possible to insert JavaScript into any web page irrespective of its file extension. You can also use JavaScript inside scripts that have been written in PHP, Perl and other languages. Therefore, JavaScript can be used in a wide range of applications.

API Availability: The availability of Application Programming Interfaces, or APIs for short, provides JavaScript with a range of functionality. This includes the setting of CSS styles, generation of audio samples and dynamic creation of HTML among others. While these APIs are built into the different web browsers, third-party APIs are also available which allow you to incorporate functionality from other web properties such as social networks like Facebook.

The Hello World Example in JavaScript

Here is the hello world example in JavaScript. This will illustrate how the language works and familiarize you with the syntax as well. As you will see, the language is quite simple.

```
<Html>

<Body>


<script language="javascript" type="text/javascript">

<!--

        document.write ("Hello World!")

        //-->
```

</script>

</body>
</html>

The Syntax in JavaScript

JavaScript is supposed to be implemented with the help of JavaScript statements. These statements are placed inside the <script>... </script> HTML tags in a web page. The <script> tags can be placed anywhere within the HTML document. The <script> tag will alert the browser to interpret the text between the tags as a script. An example of the JavaScript syntax is given below.

<script language="javascript" type="text/javascript">

Code in JavaScript

</script>

The script tag has two crucial attributes. They are given below.

Language: This attribute is used to specify which scripting language is being used. Of course, since you are using JavaScript, the value of this attribute is javascript. On the other hand, this attribute is rarely used these days for the recent versions of HTML and XHTML.

Type: This attribute is now currently being used for indicating the scripting language. The value of this attribute should be set as 'text/javascript'.

Line Breaks and Whitespace

JavaScript will ignore whitespaces. Therefore, you use newlines, tabs and spaces in your scripts freely. Of course, you should be using them to format your programs and make them look consistent and neat. This allows the code to be read and understood easily.

Semicolons

Generally, semicolons are used to mark the end of statements. This is the case in languages like Java, C++ and C. However, JavaScript makes semicolons optional in one condition. You need to ensure that each statement has been placed on a separate line. As long as you meet this condition, you can avoid inserting semicolons in the code. However, using semi-colons is a good practice especially when you are learning to program.

Case Sensitivity

You need to ensure the proper uses of cases in JavaScript as this language is case-sensitive. Therefore, all keywords, function names, variables and other identifiers must be typed with the correct case. Consistency is vital. In JavaScript, the identifiers hi and HI will have different meanings.

How to Place JavaScript in HTML Documents?

One of the good things about JavaScript is that you have the flexibility to add the code anywhere you want in an HTML document. Nonetheless, it is an excellent idea to follow the preferred methods. This can improve the readability and execution of the JavaScript code in the HTML document. Here are the best ways to include JavaScript in HTML.

Inside the <head> tags

This option is generally used when you want the script to run when an event takes place. For example, you may want the script to run when the user clicks something somewhere. In these situations, the script will be placed inside the <head> tags as shown in the following example.

<Html>

<Head>

<script type="text/javascript">

<!--

      Function sayHello () {

```
        Alert ("Hello World")

    }

    //-->
</script>


</head>


<Body>
<input type="button" onclick="sayHello ()" value="Say Hello" />
</body>


</html>
```

Inside the <body> tags

In some cases, you may need the script to run while the page loads. This is done to allow the script to generate the content located in the page. In this case, the script will have to be placed inside the <body> tags. In this method, you will not have any function that has been defined with JavaScript. You can see the example given below for such an inclusion of JavaScript.

```
<Html>


<Head>
</head>


<Body>


<script type="text/javascript">
<!--

        document.write ("Hello World")
```

```
    //-->
</script>


<p>Web Page Body </p>


</body>
</html>
```

Inside the <head> and <body> tags

If you want, you can combine the two methods above. In other words, you can place your JavaScript code inside both, the <head> and the <body> tags, in the same document. Check out the example given below to see how it works.

```
<Html>
<Head>
<script type="text/javascript">
<!--
        Function sayHello () {
          Alert ("Hello World")
        }
        //-->
</script>
</head>


<Body>
<script type="text/javascript">
<!--
        document.write ("Hello World")
        //-->
```

```
</script>
```

```
<input type="button" onclick="sayHello ()" value="Say Hello" />
```

```
</body>
</html>
```

Inside an External File

Including JavaScript inside the HTML document is a good idea when you are creating simple web pages. However, as you create websites or complex web pages, it is possible that you can find yourself reusing the same JavaScript code in multiple locations. You may even end up using the same code in multiple web pages.

As you have seen in CSS, it is possible for you to create an entirely separate file to keep your JavaScript code. You can put in all the JavaScript code that needs to be used in multiple locations or web pages inside an external file. That file should have the '.js.' extension and be associated with the web pages that require the code. The following example illustrates how an external JavaScript file can be included in an HTML document. In this example, filename.js is the file used for containing the JavaScript code.

```
<Html>
```

```
<Head>
<script type="text/javascript" src="filename.js" ></script>
</head>
```

```
<Body>
      .......
</body>
</html>
```

Data types and Variables in JavaScript

In any programming language, data types and variables are considered to be fundamental to its operation. Here is a short introduction to the data types and variables as used in JavaScript.

Data types

As you may already know, data types denote the kind of values that can be used in a programming language. There are three primitive data types available in JavaScript as mentioned below.

- Numbers
- Boolean
- Text Strings

There are two trivial data types available in JavaScript. They are undefined and null. Each of them defines a single value only.

In JavaScript, there is no difference between floating-point values and integer values. Instead, all numbers are considered to be floating-point values in JavaScript.

Variables

As you already know, variables are containers in which data can be stored. In JavaScript, a variable must be declared before it can be used in the program. You can use the var keyword to declare a variable. Look at the following example to understand how it works.

```
<script type="text/javascript">
<!--
    Var money;
    Var name;
//-->
</script>
```

In the above example, the var keyword has been used twice for declaring two variables, money and name. However, JavaScript allows multiple variables to be declared with just one var keyword. You can see this happening in the following example.

```
<script type="text/javascript">
<!--
    Var money, name;
  //-->
</script>
```

Variable initialization takes place when a value is stored in a variable. It is possible to perform variable initialization while declaring the variable in JavaScript. Alternatively, you can initialize the variable later when you require that variable. You can see this happening in the following example.

```
<script type="text/javascript">
<!--
    Var name = "John";
    Var money;
    Money = 12.30;
  //-->
</script>
```

When using variables, there are two things that you need to keep in mind.

- The var keyword must be used either for declaration or initialization. As such, it will be used only once in the lifespan of any variable in a single program. The same variable must never be declared twice, or it can result in errors.

- As JavaScript is an untied language, a variable can hold any value irrespective of the data type. In other words, you do not have to mention what kind of value that a variable should contain while it is being declared. You can change the value type of the variable during the execution. JavaScript will handle it automatically.

The Scope of Variables in JavaScript

The variable scope refers to the section of the program in which the variable is defined. Variables in JavaScript can have either one of two scopes.

Global Variables: These variables can be defined anywhere in your code due to its global scope.

Local Variables: These variables exist only inside the function that it has been defined in. Function parameters will always be local to that specific function.

In JavaScript, a local variable will be given precedence inside the body of the function if there is a global variable that has the same name. By declaring a local variable that has the same name as that of a global variable, you are effectively hiding that global variable in the function.

Rules for Variable Names

When you are giving names to your variables, you need to remember the following rules.

- The reserved keywords in JavaScript cannot be used as names for your variables.

- Variable names cannot start with a number in JavaScript. They must either start with a letter or underscore.

- As mentioned earlier, JavaScript is case sensitive. Therefore, the variable names must be used accordingly.

Events in JavaScript

An event is an action that causes a JavaScript code to be executed. Events are generally triggered by the users. For example, the click of a mouse can be an event. Based on the events, it is possible to code a response in JavaScript. For example, displaying a message can be a response to an event. These responses can be said to be the event handlers as they handle the event taking place. In JavaScript, it is possible to classify events in a number of ways. After all, there are a huge number of them.

The onClick event

The most common event type is the onClick event. This takes place whenever the user left-clicks the webpage. Against this event, you can make the appropriate response such as displaying a message or putting your validation. The following example illustrates the use of such an event for displaying a message.

```
<Html>
<Head>

<script type="text/javascript">
<!--
        Function sayHello () {
        Alert ("Hello World")
        }
        //-->
</script>

</head>

<Body>
<p>Click the following button and see result</p>

<Form>
<input type="button" onclick="sayHello ()" value="Say Hello" />
</form>

</body>
</html>
```

Conditional Statements in JavaScript

Like other programming languages, there are different kinds of conditional statements available in JavaScript. They allow you to define a condition whose results determine the action that will be done. They allow your program to make a decision based on the outcome of the condition and perform the relevant action.

If...else statement

One of the simplest and a very common conditional statement in JavaScript is the if else statement. This statement can be used in different forms.

• **If statement:** In this statement, the code will only be executed when the condition expression gives a result of true.

• **If...else statement:** Here, there will be two codes. The code under the if statement will be executed when the condition is true while the code under the else statement will be executed when the condition returns false.

• **If...else if statement:** In this statement, multiple conditions are checked instead of a single one. The condition that returns true will be executed.

The basic syntax for the if...else statement is given below.

If (expression) {

   Statement(s) to be executed if expression is true

}

Looping in JavaScript

Looping allows you to execute a single block of code multiple times till a given condition is met. JavaScript offers two kinds of loops, the for loop and the while loop.

The for loop

The for loop allows the same block of code statements to be repeatedly executed till a certain specified condition is met. The syntax of the for loop is given as follows.

For (initial expression; condition expression; loop expression)

{Statements}

The while loop

With the while loop, it becomes possible to control the number of times the loop is executed. In other words, this loop is used when you know the number of times a loop needs to be executed. As such, you need to make sure that loop is written properly so that it does not get repeated infinitely. The syntax of the while loop is given below.

While (expression) {

   Statement(s) to be executed if expression is true

}

Being an entire language, JavaScript offers a lot of other features and functions. However, you will be getting to them with time as you learn JavaScript in greater detail. Of course, you should now know how to implement a basic script written in JavaScript in your HTML web page.

Chapter 4: Build The Web With JavaScript

First of all, you should confuse JavaScript with Java. They are completely separate programming languages with no links to each other. It was originally developed in the 90s. JavaScript is one of the most necessary technologies in the development of the web as it is in use today. However, this programming language is also used in places other than a web browser such as connected services and applications.

As a programming language, JavaScript is dynamic. As a result, you have the flexibility to utilize an object-oriented programming approach or imperative and functional ones although the language is mainly object oriented. If you are already familiar with C, you will find JavaScript easier as much of the syntax is derived from the earlier programming language. In fact, it is quite easy to pick up this language. At the same time, knowledge of JavaScript can make it easier to learn Java and C.

Moreover, it is becoming very popular these days. If you are planning to become a professional coder or build things for the internet, JavaScript is one of the best languages to start with. You will be able to start building web programs quickly on learning this language.

The Features of JavaScript

JavaScript is capable of adding a variety of beautiful effects to a webpage among other things. When you are learning this programming language, it helps to understand what its features are. Here are some of the most important ones.

Browser Support

JavaScript has been accepted by all browsers as a standard scripting language. As a result, there is no need to install any plug-in to start using JavaScript in your browser, unlike Flash. More importantly, browsers provide integrated support to this language.

Client Side and Server Side Together

JavaScript can access the Document object model of a browser. As a result, it is possible to modify the structure of the WebPages at runtime. As a result, you can use this language for the addition of a variety of effects to the WebPages. At the same time, it is possible to use it on the server side. One such use is the creation of web scripts.

Scripting vs. Programming with JavaScript

JavaScript is often referred to as a scripting language because that is exactly what it is. It is not exactly a programming language per se. After all, the web browser does a lot of the work involved in the program. Since the browser does the actual work, it is possible to make changes by writing a few lines of code, which is relatively easier. This is why JavaScript is considered to be an easy language for beginners.

Nonetheless, there are some complicated aspects of this language. Even though it is employed as a scripting language, JavaScript is a thorough programming language. You can be certain write complex programs with it. Of course, this is rarely required when you are creating WebPages.

Writing a Simple Program in JavaScript

To get a better idea of JavaScript as a language, you should start writing your very first program in. The staple 'Hello World' example will be used in this case as well. The good thing is that it is very easy to write this program in JavaScript.

Before you can start, you will need to fulfill some basic requirements. One advantage of JavaScript is that it can be easily interpreted by the browser itself. As a result, you do not require any additional software or compilers for writing programs in this language. The only things you need are given below.

• **Text Editor:** You can use Notepad for writing the program. However, you should consider getting Notepad++ which is an invaluable text editor for programmers. You can get this application for free.

• **Web Browser:** You can choose any browser that you are comfortable with as all of them support JavaScript.

There is one more thing you need to do before you write the actual program and that is to create the HTML Framework. Generally, JavaScript programs will be embedded in the web page. In other words, they are written alongside the HTML. However, it is possible to include the programs externally. As such, a simply HTML file will have to be created for including the JavaScript.

To do so, open the text editor of your choice and type the following lines in the file.

<! DOCTYPE HTML>

<Html>

<Head>

<Title>JavaScript Hello World</title>

</head>

<Body>

<h1>JavaScript Hello World Example</h1>

</body>

</html>

Once done, you can save this file with a name of your choice but make sure that the file type has been designated as an HTML file. That means the file's extension should be .html and nothing else. You now have the basic template ready.

As such, you can insert the JavaScript code into the file now. Open it up and add the following lines to it. Make sure that they have been mentioned after the <h1> tag.

<Script>

<alert ("Hello World!")

<Script>

Save the file and your JavaScript program is finally ready. You can now use your web browser to run the program. Open the file in the web browser and you will see the message, 'Hello World!' being displayed.

Understanding the Syntax in JavaScript

Like all programming languages, JavaScript has its own syntax that you need to follow when writing code with it. Here are some of the most important parts of the JavaScript syntax.

<Script>

When you want to implement statements in JavaScript, you need to apply the above tag. All statements have to be placed between <script> and </script> in a web page for them to be executed. It is possible to place the <script> tags with the JavaScript code anywhere you want in a web page. However, it is a good practice to place them inside the <head> tags. The function of the <script> tag is to alert the browser to ensure that all the text between those tags is interpreted as a script. There are two important attributes to the <script> tag.

• **Language:** The language attribute will specify which scripting language is being used. Generally, the value of this attribute is JavaScript. On the other hand, the latest versions of HTML and XHTML have made it unnecessary to use this attribute.

• **Type:** Nowadays, the type attribute is recommended when you wish to mention which scripting language is being used. You should set its value to *'text/JavaScript'*.

Line Breaks and Whitespace

Unlike other programming languages, JavaScript does not pay attention to spaces, new-lines, and tabs in its programs. Since they are ignored, you can use these breaks and white spaces as many times as you want without breaking the program. You can freely use them to format the programs to make the code look neat so that it can be read and understood in an easy manner.

Semicolons are Discretional

In most programming languages such as Java and C, simple statements end with a semico-lon. This is also the case in JavaScript with a major difference. They are optional in JavaS-cript as long as the statements are placed on separate lines. You must use semicolons when you are placing two statements in one line. Be that as it may, using semicolons is a good practice for beginners.

Case Sensitivity in JavaScript

JavaScript is sensitive to the cases of the words. In other words, 'Hi' and 'hi' will be treated differently by the language.

Datatypes and Variables

Like with other programming languages, it is important to understand data types and va-riables in JavaScript.

Data Types

JavaScript offers three different primitive data types. They are Numbers, Strings of text and Boolean. The Numbers data type represents both integers and floating-point. The pro-gramming language does not define them as separate data types. Instead, all numbers will be represented as floating-point values.

There are also two other data types in JavaScript. They are undefined and null. Each of these trivial data types defines a single value only. There is a composite data type in JavaScript as well, and it is called object.

Variables

As is the case with other programming languages, there are variables in JavaScript. They need to be declared before they can be used in the program. In JavaScript, the variables have to be declared with the help of the 'var' keyword. It is possible to declare multiple variables in a single statement with this keyword. The syntax for declaring a variable is given below.

Var money;

Variable initialization is quite easy in JavaScript. You can store a value in a variable as soon as it has been declared or you can do it later in the program when required. You should remember that the 'var' keyword can be used only once for a specific variable in a program.

Another thing about JavaScript is that it is an untyped language. Therefore, a variable can contain any value irrespective of its data type in JavaScript. In other words, you do not have to inform the program what kind of data the variable can hold during its declaration. Moreover, it is possible to change the value type of any variable later. JavaScript will automatically handle the changes during the execution of the program.

In JavaScript, a variable can have two different scopes. The scope defines the region of a program in which the variable is defined.

• **Local Variables:** A local variable will remain visible only inside the function where the variable has been defined in. Function parameters are always kept local to that specific function.

• **Global Variables:** These variables have a global scope. In other words, it can be defined anywhere you want in the code of the program.

You should remember that a local variable will be given precedence in a function over a global variable that has the same name. If you declare a local variable with a name inside the body of a function that is shared by a global variable, you will be hiding the global variable for that function.

As you keep learning JavaScript, you will be coming across various functions, loops, and events. Once you can master this programming language, you can seek jobs as a web developer at the very least. Alternatively, you can pick up quite a few other programming languages more easily than before

Chapter 5: Learn The Incredible Language Of Python

Python is often mentioned as one of the best programming languages for a beginner to start with. If you are an absolute newcomer to programming, this can be an excellent choice for you. Python is quite an old language having been developed in the 80s. Guido van Rossum who developed it later gave away the language as open source. It is currently taken care of by the Python Software Foundation. Python can be used freely even for commercial applications

This is generally used as a scripting language with which programmers can compose large amounts of code in a very short period of time. Of course, the code will still remain functional and easily readable. Due to its flexibility, this language is one of the most popular of all the high-level languages in use today.

However, there is one thing you must know about Python. You are not going to be starting at the basic level even when you are a beginner. On the other hand, you will be learning a number of useful things such as modularity, naming conventions and indentation, all of which can make it easier for you when you learn other programming languages. Another advantage of this language is that the developer community is thriving allowing you to get a range of resources to help you learn Python.

Features of Python

Python is quite a powerful object-oriented programming language. It has some excellent features to offer to the programmer

• **Ease:** The ease of using Python showcases itself in multiple ways. There are fewer keywords in this language along with a clear syntax and simple structure. As a result, it is easy to learn it. The code here can be read quite easily as it is clearly defined.

• **Portability:** It is possible to run this language on a range of hardware platforms. At the same time, it will have the same interface on all of them.

• **Extendibility:** It is possible to add low-level modules to the interpreter in Python. With them, you can customize your tools or add new functions so that the tools become more efficient.

• **GUI Programming:** One of the best things about Python is that it can support GUI applications. These can be created and then ported to many windows systems and system calls including Macintosh and UNIX's X Window system.

• **Scalability:** With Python, you get a better support and structure for larger programs.

• **Interactive Mode:** In Python, you can get an interactive mode. It enables interactive debugging and testing of your code snippets easily.

- **Multiple Approaches:** While Python is mainly an object oriented programming language, it is possible to use other programming approaches such as structured and functional.

- **Other Features:** Python offers very high-level dynamic data types. Apart from supporting dynamic type checking, it also offers automatic garbage collection. Moreover, you can integrate Python with other programming languages such Java, C++ and C easily.

A Simple Program in Python

Before you can write a Python program, you need to install it on your computer. You will also get a program called IDLE. This is short for Integrated Development Environment. This is known as IDE for short in other programming languages. IDLE looks a lot similar to a basic text editor. On opening IDLE, you need to put in the following command at the prompt.

print ("Hello, World!")

As you can see, the code for a Hello World program in Python is much shorter than the other programming languages that you have seen so far. This is one of the reasons for the popularity of this language. You can even easily understand what is happening in the code.

Data Types and Variables

Understanding the variables and data types will certainly help you out when you are learning Python.

Data Types

In Python, all values have a data type. Moreover, everything is considered to be an object in this programming language. Therefore, data types are actually considered to be classes while variables are considered to be instances of the respective classes. Here are some of the most important data types in Python.

- **Python Numbers:** In this category, you will find floating point numbers, complex numbers, and integers. In Python, they are defined as a float, complex, and int. It is possible to discover the class of the variable with the type () function. The *instance ()* function can be used to check whether an object belongs to a specified class.

- **Python List:** As the name suggests, List is an ordered series of items. It is one of the most widely used data types and is rather flexible. In Python, the items of a list can belong to different data types. The value of the items in a list can be changed as per requirements. Therefore, the list is mutable.

- **Python Tuple:** Tuple is similar to a list as it also has an ordered series of items. However, a tuple is immutable. Therefore, the values in a tuple cannot be modified once it has been created. They are mainly used for write-protecting data.

Variables

While the function of variables in Python is the same as the other programming languages, there is a difference in their declaration. In Python, you do not have to declare a variable before using it. You simply need to assign a value to the variable, and it will exist. You do not have to define the data type of the variable as well. Python will define the data type automatically based on the value assigned to the variable.

Naming the variables properly is essential in Python. The names can be a combination of letters in uppercase and smaller case along with digits and underscore. However, a name cannot start with a number. Special symbols cannot be used for naming variables. You cannot use keywords for the names as well. These rules are also applicable when you are writing identifiers.

Conditional Statements and Loops

Like other programming languages, Python also offers a range of conditional statements to help your program make decisions and loops for executing a code multiple times.

Conditional Statements

There are a few conditional statements available in Python. In this programming language, a null or a zero value is considered to be TRUE while any non-null or non-zero value is taken to be False.

- **If statements:** In this conditional statement, the block of code under the statement will be executed when the if expression returns TRUE. If FALSE, the execution of that code will be skipped and the statement after it will be executed.

- **If else statements:** These statements contain an else statement after the if statement. The block of code under the else statement will be executed when the if expression is determined to be FALSE.

- **If elif else statements:** The elif statement is used to check multiple conditions and expressions. When one of the given conditions is determined to be TRUE, a block of code associated with that elif statement will be executed. As such, there can be multiple elif statements following an if statement. The block of code executed corresponds to the elif statement which was evaluated to TRUE.

Loops

Loops in Python are similar to other programming languages.

- **While loop:** This loop allows you to repeat the execution of a block of code as long as the specified condition is TRUE. The condition will be tested every time before the body of the loop is executed.

- **For loop:** The for loop also allows you to execute a block of code. However, it keeps the code required for managing the loop variable short.

Like other programming languages, it is also possible to create nested loops in Python.

Learning Python can certainly open up a plethora of opportunities. More importantly, once you become adept in Python, you will find programming easier in general.

Nearly all of the applications that are used by a person on a daily basis communicate with various servers to work. For an application to do this successfully, it will have to be programmed correctly. If a request is not processed correctly, it will usually lead to a variety of errors. In this first chapter, we are going to cover some of the basics of programming and why they have to be learned when trying to achieve success with the program.

Breaking Down the Function of an Application

The first thing that you will need to do when trying to be a successful programmer is how to break down what an application does. To be a good Python Programmer, you will need to become familiar with the order of operations required to make a program work. The best way to get experience with this process is by making a list of what needs to work in an application and what operations have to be laid out for this to happen.

By getting familiar with this breaking down of operations, you will be able to get an application built without having complications that compromise its functionality. You need to be aware that computers are made to perform precisely what they are programmed to do. This means that if there are any mistakes, then the computer will not be able to compensate for them. Due to this fact, you will have to be meticulous in regards to the commands that you give to the computer. A computer is inflexible in regards to the way it obeys commands, which puts all of the responsibility on you to input the right Python Programming to ensure the application you design is correct.

The Special Language of Computers

The language of computers is also something that you will need to become very familiar with. You will not be able just to tell a computer to check an email or show an individual screen when a link is clicked; you have to learn how to speak their language. There have been many different types of coding used over the years, and each of them seems more complicated than the next. Using bits of binary code will help to turn parts of a computer's processor on and off with ease. The whole purpose behind Python Programming is to make it easy for you to develop applications without having to complicate matters like C++ code can do. The lines of code that are produced by Python are very easy to read and to alter when needed. When using a coding discipline like C++, a beginner will find it nearly impossible to figure out what the lines of code say and how to work within them to create what they want. The primary goal of any application is to allow users to communicate with their computers in a new way. Your job as a programmer will allow you to open up a whole new world for people when it comes to using their computers.

Things to Consider When Working on a New Application

When working on a new application, you will usually have a variety of different roadblocks to address along the way. When first starting out in the world of Python Programming, you will have a bit of a learning curve. The more you can work on various applications, the easier you will find it to become familiar with the programming process. Following a few ground rules will allow you to perfect an application without a lot of effort being invested in the process.

The first thing you need to consider when attempting to develop an application is what you find distracting about it. For most programmers, developing applications that are straightforward and easy to use is critical. By taking the time to simplify the application you are working on, you will be able to eliminate the confusion that a user may have. One of the first things that you will need to do when starting an application is to set the date and time in order to do this, you will need to do the following:

- Open a Blank file

- Save it as dateparser.py

- Use the following code to set time and date

```
from datetime import datetime

now = datetime.now()

mm = str(now.month)

dd = str(now.day)

yyyy = str(now.year)

hour = str(now.hour)

mi = str(now.minute)

ss = str(now.second)

print mm + "/" + dd + "/" + yyyy + " " + hour + ":" + mi + ":" + ss
```

Once you have this in the file, you will need to save it and exit. Once you are ready to put these changes in your application, you will need to run it. In some cases, you may want to use the time.sleep function to provide a time break within an application. Most programmers want to use this break in 5 second intervals. Below you will find the coding you need to activate this time sleep within your application.

import time

time.sleep(5)

The number in the parenthesis is the number of seconds the time sleep will be active for. You can change this number in order to find the right delay that works for the particular part of your application. If you want to avoid having to input all of the numbers regarding time and date, the following Python coding will allow you to get the current time and date settings for your application.

import datetime

now = datetime.datetime.now()

print

print "Current date and time using str method of datetime object:"

print str(now)

print

print "Current date and time using instance attributes:"

print "Current year: %d" % now.year

print "Current month: %d" % now.month

print "Current day: %d" % now.day

print "Current hour: %d" % now.hour

print "Current minute: %d" % now.minute

print "Current second: %d" % now.second

print "Current microsecond: %d" % now.microsecond

print

print "Current date and time using strftime:"

print now.strftime("%Y-%m-%d %H:%M")

Another thing to think about when attempting to perfect an application is easy to use elements it has. Once an application has been built, you will need to give it a test run. During this trial run, you will need to think more like a user than a programmer. Be sure to make notes as to what parts of the application were easiest to use and which ones gave you trouble. By doing this type of assessment, you can fix the bugs that you find with ease.

The last thing you will need to contemplate when attempting to fine tune an application is whether or not it did the job it was intended for. If the app looks great and has impressive graphics, but does not do the job it needs to, then you will need to go back to the drawing board. The bells and whistles that are on an app will only go so far. The last thing that you want is to have people growing tired of your app after only a few uses. Having an application that is functional is far better than having a program than just looks good. There is a gray area that will allow you to have both of these elements. Your job is to find this middle ground and use it to your advantage.

Reasons Why Python is So Popular

The main thing that most people will want to know when getting into this type of programming is why it is so popular. There are so many different programming languages out there. Each of them is created with a simple goal of communicating with computers better, but this is not always the result. Many of the programming languages out there are so challenging and complicated to use that it ends up frustrating a user and making them give up on their dream of being a computer program. The whole reasoning behind the Python Programming method was to provide an easy to use language for programmers to use in any application.

One of the biggest reasons for the popularity of Python is that it allows more to be done in a shorter amount of time. Because more can be done with fewer lines of Python code, it takes far less time to develop an application. For the computer programmer looking to churn out multiple applications in a day, Python is just the right fit. Most developers consider the use of Python as a no-brainer due to the amount of time it saves and the versatility that it has. Rather than toiling away for hours on end with Java or C++, you can do the same thing with Python in half of the time.

The next reason why Python is so popular is that it helps you to create code that is very easy to read. To work within a code and tweak, you will have to be able to read it quickly. The primary goal of Python Programming developers was to make their code the easiest to read out of all of the coding languages out there. Because this code is so easy to read, it will take you far less time to scan it and make the changes needed. When using coding languages like Java, you will spend hours going through each line of code. Even the smallest error in coding can make an application malfunction. Using Python allows you to find mistakes in a hurry and correct them before any problems occur.

Due to the simplicity of the Python coding system, the time it takes to learn it is significantly reduced. You will not have to worry about perfecting odd rules to have success with this coding language. Many people who have a bit of experience in coding will be able to start using Python right away. Being able to hit the ground running with this type of coding will allow you to get applications made in no time. If you are looking to start your programming career in a hurry, then the only logical choice you have is to learn Python.

The versatility that Python has is also a big selling point for most people. This coding language can be used in browser-based applications and XML. If you are into developing user interfaces or even interacting with other databases, you will be able to use Python to do so with ease. After you have perfected the art of Python Programming, you will be able to use it in any application development process. Having this versatility will allow you to take on a variety of jobs in some different industries.

Now that you know all about why people use computer code, you are ready to delve in deeper to the world of Python Programming. In the next chapter, you will learn how to get a copy of Python for your system and how to download it properly. By having your copy of

Python, you will be able to work with it and figure out how to use it for your application development.

To create programs using this type of programming method, you will have to get an application to enter the code into. There is an alternative to getting an application like this, which is writing the application using what is called machine code. This process is a tough one and may lead to you becoming frustrated and giving up on this task altogether. The applications out there made for Python will allow you to type in the code and run it to see what it does in real time. This means that you will be able to find and address mistakes with ease when downloading these programs. In this chapter, you will be able to find out how to get these programs and how best to use them for your particular needs.

Understanding the Platform

Before you can start to use these programs, you will need to understand what a platform is. The short explanation of a platform is the combination of the computer's hardware with an operating system. A platform will have specialized rules that dictate how it will run. The details of how a platform runs will be hidden from you in the Python application. This means that as you type in the code, the Python application will turn it into something that can be used by the platform as a layout. Making this program work successfully will require you to find a Python version that works for the particular operating system that you are running.

Due to the overwhelming number of platforms out there, you will have to invest some time and effort into getting the right Python program. By going here, you will be able to get a list of different downloads. The main part of this page will have links for the most popular downloads like Mac, Windows or Linux. There is a list of links on the left of the screen that give you alternate Python settings to use if needed. If you are looking for a more updated editor than what comes in the regular download, you will be able to find it in these alternate settings. Regardless of what platform you are using, you will be able to find a Python program that works for it.

Installing the Python Program

Once you have found the download that will work for your platform, you will be ready to install it on your computer. Here is what you will need to do to install on the various operating systems out there.

Windows and other Similar Systems

If you are using the Windows or similar operating systems, you will need first to find the file that you have downloaded from the Python site. The name of the file will vary, but you can usually find it by searching the word Python in your folder search box. Once you have found this download, you will need to double click it to get started. Usually, a dialog box will pop and ask you if you are sure you want to run this file. You will click run to get the process started. After you click run, the wizard program will guide you through what you need to do to get the program going. This program will ask you where you want to put the files downloaded from the Python program. Creating a specific folder for this program and placing all of the records there is the best way to be able to keep up with them. You can do a custom install where you put the various files in different locations, but this takes a lot of time and is usually not necessary. Running the program on the Windows system will be easy when using the Command Prompt option. When opening Command Prompt, you will be able to type in Python to get the program to come up.

Using the Mac System

If you are a fan of all things Apple, then chances are you are using a Mac rather than a PC. Python has a version that is compatible with the Mac, which means you should have no problem getting it installed. Once you have downloaded the file, you will need to double-click it and start the process of getting it on your computer. When you initiate this download process, you will be asked to put in your administrator password. Once you see the Install Succeeded dialog box, you will be able to start using your new Python program.

In any programming language, variables and data types are two of the most important concepts you will come across. After all, variables form an integral part to all complex programs.

What are Variables?

Variables are simply memory locations that have been reserved for the storage of values. In other words, you will actually be reserving some space in the memory when you create a variable.

The interpreter will allocate memory to the variable based on its data type. It will also decide what can be stored in that specific reserved memory with the help of the data type. Therefore, you can store decimals, characters or integers in these variables by assigning the right data type to the variable.

Assigning Values to a Variable in Python

In Python, you do not need to explicitly declare a variable in order to reserve space in the memory unlike other programming languages. Instead, the declaration will take place automatically when a value has been assigned to a variable. In order to assign a value to the variable, the equal sign is used. The operand located to the left of the = operator will be the name of your variable. The operand located to the right of this operator will be the value that you wish to store in the variable.

The following example shows how you can assign values to different variables in Python.

```
#! /usr/bin/python


Counter = 100      # an integer assignment
```

Miles = *1000.0*   *# A floating point*

Name = *"John"*   *# A string*

Print counter

Print miles

Print name

As you can see in the above example, counter, name and miles are all variables while the values that they have been assigned are 100, John and 1000.0 respectively. On executing the code shown above, the following result will be produced.

100

1000.0

John

Assigning Multiple Variables in Python

There is no need to use multiple statements for assigning values to variables in Python. There are different ways by which this can be achieved.

You can certainly take a single value and get it assigned to multiple variables at the same time. In order to know how to accomplish this, take a look at the following example shown below.

a = *b* = *c* = *1*

On the other hand, you can also assign different values to different variables at the same time. You simply need to make sure that each consecutive object has been separated by means of a comma. You can even assign different values of different data types simultaneously. The following example shows you can do this.

A, b, c = 1, 2, "john"

The Standard Datatypes in Python

The fact is that you can store data of different types in memory. Take the example of a person. The age of the person will be numeric but the name will be only alphabetic. On the other hand, the address of the person will consist of alphanumeric numbers. That is why Python offers a range of standard data types which can be used for defining the operations that are possible on them. The data types also determine the storage method available for the variable.

There are quite a few data types available in Python. Some of them are listed below.

- Numbers
- List
- String
- Tuple
- Dictionary

We will be taking a look at each of these data types in greater detail in turn. However, there is one little thing that you should know first.

Conversion of Datatypes in Python

There can be a number of situations in which you need to convert a particular variable from one data type to another. In order to perform a conversion between types, you simply have to use the name of the data type as a function. There are a number of built-in functions in Python which allow you to convert a variable from one data type to another. These functions will return a new object that represents the converted value. Take a look at the functions as shown below.

Int(x [, base])

This will convert x into an integer. Here, base specifies what the base will be if x happens to be a string.

Long(x [, base])

This will be converting x into a long integer. As with string, base states what the base will be when x is actually a string.

Float(x)

This will be converting x into a floating-point number.

Complex (real [, imag])

This will create a complex number

STR(x)

This will convert object x into its string representation.

repr(x)

This is going to convert object x into an expression string.

eval(str)

This will take the string and evaluate it and then return an object.

tuple(s)

This will convert s into a tuple.

List

It will be converting s into a list.

Set

This will be converting s into a set.

Dict (d)

This will create a dictionary. In this case, d has to be a sequence of tuples with key and values.

Frozenset

Here, s will be converted into a frozen set.

Chr(x)

This will convert an integer into a character. In this case, x is the integer.

Unichr(x)

Here, x has to be an integer. It will be converted into a Unicode character.

Ord(x)

This will be converting a single character into its integer value.

Hex(x)

Here, an integer will be converted into a hexadecimal string.

Oct(x)

This will be converting an integer into an octal string.

Now that data type conversions are over with, let us take a detailed look at the different data types available in Python.

Number Datatypes in Python

As the name suggests, number data types will be storing numeric values. This data type is immutable. In other words, if you change the value of a number data type object, and entirely new object will be allocated. You can easily create a number object by assigning a value to them.

The following example shows you how you can assign a number variable.

var1 = 1

var2 = 10

It is also possible to delete the reference to any number object by means of the Del statement. The syntax for this statement is given below.

Del var1 [, var2 [, var3 [...., varN]]]

The Del statement can also be used for deleting a single object or even multiple objects. The following example shows you can do it.

Del var

Del var_a, var_b

Kinds of Numerical Datatypes

Python offers support for four different kinds of numerical data types. They are as follows.

Int: These are called either integers or ints. They are signed integers and they can be either positive or negative. They are whole numbers and do not have any decimal point.

Long: These are long integers and they are often referred to as longs. These integers can be of unlimited size. They are written in the same way like integers but are followed by an L in the lowercase or the uppercase.

Float: They are floating point real values and are also called floats. These are representative of real numbers and they will be written with a decimal point that divides the integer and the fractional parts. Floats can also be written in scientific notation. E or e will be used to indicate the power of 10.

Complex: They are complex numbers and their form is "a + bJ". Here, a and b will be floats while J is representative of the square root of -1 which is, of course, an imaginary number. Complex numbers are rarely used while programming in Python.

Converting From One Number Type to Another

Python is capable of converting the numbers internally in expressions that contain mixed types to a common type for the sake of evaluation. However, there can be situations in which the number has to be explicitly converted from one number type to another. This is usually done so as to fulfill the requirements of a function parameter or an operator.

The statements that can be used for this purpose are given below.

* int(x)

This will convert x into a plain integer.

* long(x)

This will convert x into a long integer.

* float(x)

This will convert x into a floating-point number.

* complex(x)

This will convert x into a complex number. The real part will be x while the imaginary part will be zero.

- complex(x, y)

This will convert x and y into a complex number. The real part will be x while the imaginary part will be y. In this case, both x and y will be numeric expressions.

String Datatypes in Python

Of all the data types available in Python, strings are easily the most popular. They can be easily created by using quotes for enclosing a few characters. In Python, single quotes are given the same treatment as double quotes. In other words, they are the same. It is quite easy to create a string. All you need to do is assign a value to a variable. Take a look at the example given below.

var1 = 'Hello World!'

var2 = "Python Programming"

Accessing the Values in a String

The fact is that Python does not have a character data type. Instead, they are considered to be strings that have a length of one. As a result, they also considered to be a substring. In order to access the substrings, you should be using the square brackets with the index so as to slice them and get the substring that you require.

The following example shows how you can access the value in any string.

#! /usr/bin/python

var1 = 'Hello World!'

var2 = "Python Programming"

Print "var1 [0]: "var1 [0]

Print "var2 [1:5]: "var2 [1:5]

After executing the code shown above, you will find the result to be the same as shown below.

var1 [0]: H

var2 [1:5]: ytho

Updating the Values in Strings

It is possible to update a string that already exists by re-assigning a variable to a different string. The new value that you get can be related to the previous value that you have or it can be a completely new and different string. Regard the following example to understand how strings can be updated.

#! /usr/bin/python

var1 = 'Hello World!'

Print "Updated String: - ", var1 [:6] + 'Python'

On executing the code shown in the above example, the following result can be derived.

Updated String: - Hello Python

String Formatting Operator in Python

The string format operator is % in Python and it happens to be one of the best features of this language. The operator is completely unique to strings. There are quite a few symbols that can be used with the % operator.

The following example shows how this operator can be used.

#! /usr/bin/python

Print "My name is %s and weight is %d kg!" % ('John', 21)

After executing the code show in the above example, the result that you will notice is given as follows.

My name is John and weight is 21 kg!

Use of Triple Quotes

The triple quotes available in Python serve a very useful purpose. With them, you can let your strings be written over multiple lines including TABs, newlines and other special characters. You should already be familiar with triple quotes as shown earlier in the book.

The following example illustrates the use of triple quotes.

#! /usr/bin/python

para_str = """this is a long string that is made up of

Several lines and non-printable characters such as

TAB (\t) and they will show up that way when displayed.

NEWLINEs within the string, whether explicitly given like

This within the brackets [\n], or just a NEWLINE within

The variable assignment will also show up.

"""

Print para_str

On executing the code shown above, the result produced is shown below.

This is a long string that is made up of

Several lines and non-printable characters such as

TAB (   ) and they will show up that way when displayed.

NEWLINEs within the string, whether explicitly given like

This within the brackets [

], or just a NEWLINE within

The variable assignment will also show up.

As you can see, all special characters have been converted to their printed equivalents without any errors. You should also remember that newlines can occur with an explicit carriage return present at the end of the line. Alternatively, the escape code of newlines (\n) can be used for this purpose.

Raw Strings

Raw strings will not consider the backslash to be a special character. Instead, all characters placed inside the raw string will remain the same without any change. Check out the following set of examples.

#! /usr/bin/python

Print 'C: \\nowhere'

As you can see, this is not a raw string. As a result, it will end up producing the result shown below.

C:\nowhere

The example given below, however, does make use of raw string. See how the r'expression' has been used.

#! /usr/bin/python

Print r'C:\\nowhere'

On executing the code shown above, the result produced is given below. As you will notice, the string has not undergone any change unlike the previous example.

C:\\nowhere

So far, we have learned about the number and the string data types in Python, what they are and how they can be used. There are three other data types that you should know about but we shall be tackling them in the next chapter.

The sequence is the most basic of all the data structures available in Python. In a sequence, each element will be assigned a number which denotes its index or its position. The first index will always be zero while the second index will be one and this way it will go on.

There are six types of sequences that have been built into Python. However, the most commonly used ones are lists and tuples. They are the ones you should know about at the moment. You will learn about the others as you progress into the more advanced stages of learning Python.

There are quite a few operations that can be done with all the sequence types. Those operations include slicing, indexing, adding and multiplying among others. Additionally, built-in functions are available in Python that allow you to find the larges and smallest elements in a sequence as well as its length.

Lists in Python

Lists are the most versatile of all the data types available in Python. It can be written as a sequence of values or items separated by means of commas and located between square brackets. One of the most important features of lists is that the items present in the list can be of varying data types.

The following example shows how you can create lists. As you will see, it is very easy to make a list.

list1 = ['physics', 'chemistry', 1997, 2000];

list2 = [1, 2, 3, 4, 5];

list3 = ["a", "b", "c", "d"]

Accessing the Values in a List

If you want to access the values present in a list, you need to use the square brackets to slice along with the indices so as to get the value present at that specific index. Take the following example into account.

#! /usr/bin/python

list1 = ['physics', 'chemistry', 1997, 2000];

list2 = [1, 2, 3, 4, 5, 6, 7];

Print "list1 [0]: "list1 [0]

Print "list2 [1:5]: "list2 [1:5]

After you execute the code shown above, the result that will be shown is given below.

list1 [0]: physics

list2 [1:5]: [2, 3, 4, and 5]

Updating a List in Python

It is possible to update single and even multiple items present in a list. You simply need to give the slice on the left side of the assignment operator. The following example shows how you can do so.

#! /usr/bin/python

List = ['physics', 'chemistry', 1997, 2000];

Print "Value available at index 2:"

Print list [2]

List [2] = 2001;

Print "New value available at index 2:"

Print list [2]

After executing the code shown above, the result that will be produced is shown below.

Value available at index 2:

1997

New value available at index 2:

2001

Deleting Elements in a List

It is possible to remove a single or even multiple elements from a list. However, the procedure depends on whether you know which element you wish to remove. If you do know the exact element that needs to be removed, the Del statement can be used. If you do not know, then the remove () method will have to be used.

The following example shows how the Del statement can be used.

```
#! /usr/bin/python

list1 = ['physics', 'chemistry', 1997, 2000];

Print list1
Del list1 [2];
Print "After deleting value at index 2:"
Print list1
```

On executing the code in the example shown above, the following result will be displayed.

```
['Physics', 'chemistry', 1997, 2000]
After deleting value at index 2:
['Physics', 'chemistry', 2000]
```

Tuples in Python

Like lists, tuples are also sequences of Python objects. However, the objects are immutable. As a result, it is not possible to change tuples unlike lists which can be changes whenever required. Moreover, a tuple will be using parentheses unlike lists which use square brackets. On the other hand, creating a tuple is similar to creating lists and the process is simple. You simply need to put the different values separated by a comma. Alternatively, the values separated by commas can be placed inside parentheses.

The following example illustrates how tuples can be created.

tup1 = ('physics', 'chemistry', 1997, 2000);

tup2 = (1, 2, 3, 4, 5);

tup3 = "a", "b", "c", "d";

It is also possible to create an empty tuple. You simply need to use the parentheses without placing anything inside. The following example illustrates the creation of an empty tuple.

tup1 = ();

In order to create a tuple that contains a single value only, a comma has to be included. Take a look at the following example.

tup1 = (50,);

Accessing the Values in Tuples

In order to access the values inside a tuple, you will have to use the indices for slicing them and obtain the value present at a specific index. Take a look at the example given below.

#! /usr/bin/python

tup1 = ('physics', 'chemistry', 1997, 2000);

tup2 = (1, 2, 3, 4, 5, 6, 7);

Print "tup1 [0]: "tup1 [0]

Print "tup2 [1:5]: "tup2 [1:5]

On executing the code given above, the following result will be produced.

tup1 [0]: physics

tup2 [1:5]: [2, 3, 4, and 5]

Updating Elements in Tuples

As tuples are immutable, it is not possible for you to update or modify the values of the elements present inside one. On the other hand, you can take parts of an existing tuple and then create a new tuple. The following example shows you how this can be achieved.

```
#! /usr/bin/python


tup1 = (12, 34.50),
tup2 = ('abc', 'xyz');


# following action is not valid for tuples
# tup1 [0] = 100;


# So let's create a new tuple as follows
tup3 = tup1 + tup2;
Print tup3
```

The following result is produced when the code given above is executed.

(12, 34.56, 'abc', 'xyz')

Deleting Elements in Tuple

Again, it is not possible to remove individual or multiple elements in a tuple because of the immutable nature of tuples. On the other hand, you can create a new tuple by adding all the elements that you want from the previous tuple while skipping out the ones that you wanted to get rid of. This process is rather easy and you already know how you can extract specific elements out of a tuple.

Of course, you can easily remove an entire tuple if you want. To explicitly remove tuples, the Del statement can be used. The following example demonstrates this action.

#! /usr/bin/python

Tup = ('physics', 'chemistry', 1997, 2000);

Print tup

Del tup;

Print "After deleting tup:"

Print tup

The result produced on executing the code shown in the above example is given as follows. You will notice that an exception has been raised. This is due to the fact that the tuple tup does not exist anymore once the Del statement has been executed.

('Physics', 'chemistry', 1997, 2000)

After deleting tup:

Traceback (most recent call last):

  File "test.py", line 9, in <module>

    Print tup;

NameError: name 'tup' is not defined

Dictionaries in Tuple

The dictionary data type in Python can be said to be a hash table type. If you are familiar with Perl, you will notice that they tend to work like hashes or associative arrays. A dictionary is enclosed by means of curly braces while its elements can be assigned or accessed by means of square braces.

An element in a Python dictionary consists of a pair of key and value. Any data type in this programming language can be used for the dictionary key as long as they are immutable. Therefore, the data types used for the key are numbers, strings or tuples. On the other hand, values can be any arbitrary object in Python. Each key will be separated from its associated value with the help of a colon (:) while the elements are separated with the help of commas. In any dictionary, the keys in it will always be unique but the values may not be.

Accessing the Values in a Dictionary

The process to access the elements present in a dictionary is similar to what you have done for lists and strings. You need to use the square brackets. However, instead of indices, you will be using the key so as to obtain the value. The following example shows you how you can do so.

```
#! /usr/bin/python

Dict = {'Name': 'Zara', 'Age': 7, 'Class': 'First'}

Print "dict ['Name']: "dict ['Name']
Print "dict ['Age']: "dict ['Age']
```

On executing the code shown above, the following result will be produced.

```
Dict ['Name']: Zara
Dict ['Age']: 7
```

You must make sure that you are trying to access the element with the right key. If you try to use a key that is not a part of the dictionary an error will be shown. Take a look at the following example.

```
#! /usr/bin/python
```

Dict = {'Name': 'Zara', 'Age': 7, 'Class': 'First'}

Print "dict ['Alice']: "dict ['Alice']

Upon executing the code given above, you will find the following result has been produced.

Dict ['Alice']:

Traceback (most recent call last):

  File "test.py", line 4, in <module>

    Print "dict ['Alice']: "dict ['Alice'];

KeyError: 'Alice'

Updating the Dictionary

It is possible to update the dictionary easily. You can add a new pair of key and value. You can also change an existing entry or even delete an existing entry. The process is illustrated in the example shown below.

```
#! /usr/bin/python
```

Dict = {'Name': 'Zara', 'Age': 7, 'Class': 'First'}

Dict ['Age'] = 8; # update existing entry

Dict ['School'] = "DPS School"; # Add new entry

Print "dict ['Age']: "dict ['Age']

Print "dict ['School']: "dict ['School']

After executing the code shown in the above example, the following result will be produced.

Dict ['Age']: 8

Dict ['School']: DPS School

Deleting the Elements in a Dictionary

It is possible to remove individual elements in a dictionary in Python. Alternatively, you can get rid of all the elements present in the dictionary. Of course, the entire dictionary can be deleted and that too in a single operation. The Del statement can be used for explicitly removing the entire dictionary. The following example demonstrates how this will be possible.

```
#! /usr/bin/python

Dict = {'Name': 'Zara', 'Age': 7, 'Class': 'First'}

Del dict ['Name']; # remove entry with key 'Name'
dict.clear ();    # remove all entries in dict
Del dict;        # delete entire dictionary

Print "dict ['Age']: "dict ['Age']
Print "dict ['School']: "dict ['School']
```

The execution of the above code will cause the following results to be displayed. You will notice that an exception will be raised. This is because the dictionary dict does not exist once the Del statement has been executed.

Dict ['Age']:

Traceback (most recent call last):

  File "test.py", line 8, in <module>

    Print "dict ['Age']: "dict ['Age'];

TypeError: 'type' object is unsubscriptable

The Properties of the Dictionary Keys

The values present in a dictionary do not have any restrictions. You can use any arbitrary Python object. They can be user-defined objects or standard objects. On the other hand, the keys of the dictionaries need to follow some important rules. Those rules are given below.

Duplicate Keys Not Allowed: It is not possible to have more than one entry for each keyword. Therefore, there cannot be any duplicate keys in your dictionary. If duplicate keys are encountered during assignment, it will be the last assignment that gets the preference.

#! /usr/bin/python

Dict = {'Name': 'Zara', 'Age': 7, 'Name': 'Mani'}

Print "dict ['Name']: "dict ['Name']

On executing the code given in the above example, you will find the following result has been produced.

Dict ['Name']: Mani

Keys Must Always Be Immutable: You have to ensure that the keys chosen are of an immutable nature. Therefore, the data types that you can use as dictionary keys are numbers, tuples and strings. Check the following example to get a better understanding.

```
#! /usr/bin/python

Dict = {['Name']: 'Zara', 'Age': 7}

Print "dict ['Name']: "dict ['Name']
```

The following result is produced on executing the code given in the above example.

```
Traceback (most recent call last):
   File "test.py", line 3, in <module>
     Dict = {['Name']: 'Zara', 'Age': 7};
TypeError: list objects are unhashable
```

Chapter 6: Enjoy the Ease of Ruby

Developed in the 90s, Ruby is one of the most recent programming languages in the world. Even so, it is remarkably popular thanks to its dynamic and open-source nature. It is an object-oriented programming language which was designed to possess an easily readable syntax that could be written even by a beginner. There is no need to learn and memorize a huge list of commands to get started with Ruby.

Ruby is known to be a programming language that is quite easy to learn. In fact, it is possible to pick up the basics in less than an hour. You can find a quick start guide that will take around 20 minutes to complete by the end of which you will be acquainted with the fundamentals of this programming language. If you are already familiar with Python, learning Ruby will become less of a challenge.

Another thing you need to keep in mind is the difference between Ruby on Rails and Ruby. You see, Ruby is a programming language. On the other hand, Ruby on Rails is a framework that has been built with Ruby. While Ruby is a general purpose scripting language, Ruby on Rails allows the development of web applications.

The Features of Ruby

There are some excellent features in Ruby that make it a useful programming language to learn. Here are some of the top features.

Flexibility: Although Ruby is an object-oriented programming language, it also provides support for imperative, functional and procedural programming. As a result, it is quite flexible for many programming requirements.

Objects: In Ruby, you will find that everything is considered to be an object. This also applies to numeric values. This greatly simplifies programming in this language.

Blocks: One of the best features of Ruby is the blocks. These are blocks of code which can be used as a parameter in a method. This greatly simplifies Ruby programming allowing you to build code libraries easily. These libraries can be used to provide various functionalities to code blocks that you build later.

Scalability: This is another excellent feature in Ruby. You can easily maintain programs written in this language even they are quite big.

A Simple Program in Ruby

As with other programming languages, here is the basic Hello World example program written in the Ruby language.

```
#! /usr/bin/ruby -w


puts "Hello, World!"
```

As you can see in the example, the program is incredibly simple with only a single line of actual code. This goes on to show how easy it is to learn and write programs in this language.

The Syntax in Ruby Programming

In any programming language, you need to pay attention to the syntax of the code. Improper syntax can cause errors during runtime or even break the program and give results that are different from what is expected. In Ruby, the syntax concepts are quite simple and easy to understand. Here is some of the syntax concepts that you need to know when programming in this language.

Whitespace

In Ruby, whitespace characters such as tabs and spaces are typically ignored by the program. However, they will be taken into account when they are present in strings. Be that as it may, there are certain cases in which white spaces are used for interpreting ambiguous statements. These interpretations can produce warnings if the –w option has been enabled.

Line Endings

In Ruby, newline characters and semicolons are treated as the ending of statements. However, if operators like backslash and + are placed at the end of a line, Ruby will treat them as an indicator that the statement is going to be continued.

Identifiers

Identifiers are the names given to methods, constants and variables. In Ruby, identifiers are always case sensitive. Therefore, 'Hi', 'HI' and 'hi' will be treated as different identifiers in Ruby. On the other hand, you can make use of alphanumeric characters as well as the underscore character in making your identifiers.

BEGIN and END Statements in Ruby

These are two important statements in Ruby. You are certain to come across situations where you need to use these statements as you program in this language.

The BEGIN Statement

This statement allows the code under it to be declared before the actual program is executed. Therefore, the code in the BEGIN statement will be the first to be executed. You can use multiple BEGIN statements, and they will be executed in the order they appear in the program. The basic syntax of this statement is given below.

BEGIN {

#code

}

The END Statement

This is the opposite of the BEGIN statement as the code it declares will be executed at the end of the program. The syntax for this statement is given below.

END {

#code

}

Variables in Ruby

There are four different kinds of variables in Ruby. Understanding them is vital to Ruby programming. Here is a short introduction to these variables.

Class Variables: As the name suggests, these variables belong to a specific class and are available to the different objects in that class. It is also a characteristic of that class. They will be shared among the descendants of the module or the class in which they were defined. You need to initialize them before you can use them in method definitions. If the -w option is usedthen; warnings will be produced when the class variable is overridden. All class variables have to start with @@.

Instance Variables: These variables will be available for different methods for a specific object or instance. Therefore, instance variables will be different for different objects. If uninitialized, the instance variable will have the value of nil and it will cause warnings if the -w option has been used. All instance variables will have to start to @.

Local Variables: The scope of these variables range from the start of a block of code to its end. In other words, it exists between the braces. They are not available outside the method. If you reference an uninitialized local variable, Ruby will consider it to be a call to a method which has no arguments. It is possible to declare local variables by assigning to uninitialized local variables. All local variables have to start with either an underscore or with a lowercase letter.

Global Variables: These variables are used when you need to have a variable that can exist for all classes. By assigning to global variables, you can change the global status. As such, their usage is not recommended unless absolutely necessary. They can complicate the program. Uninitialized global variables will have the value of nil. With the -w option, they can cause warnings. All global variables need to start with the '$' character.

Conditional Structures in Ruby

There are quite a few conditional structures available in Ruby, most of which are common to other programming languages. Therefore, you should not have a problem if you are familiar with other languages. Even if you do not, it will not be difficult for you to learn.

• **If statement:** This statement is used to execute a block of code when a condition is determined to be true. The execution of the code will be skipped when the condition returns false.

• **Else statement:** The else statement is used with the if statement. It provides an alternate block of code to be executed when the condition is evaluated false.

• **Elsif statement:** The elsif statement is used with the if and else statements and is put between the two. It is possible to add as many elsif statements as required. This statement is used when you need multiple conditions to be checked. The elsif statement which returns true for the condition will have its block of code executed.

• **Unless statement:** The unless statement is the opposite of the if statement. It used when you want a block of code to be executed when the condition returns false.

• **Case when statement:** Using the if-elsif-else conditional structure can get quite complicated when you need to evaluate a lot of options. In these situations, you can apply the case when statement. The code under the when statement will be executed when the condition returns the right value. Multiple when statements can be applied to a case statement. It is also possible to use the else statement with this conditional structure. The else statement will give a block of code to be executed when the condition does not return any value acceptable to the when statements.

Loop Statements in Ruby

Loops are also available in Ruby. As you already know, loops allow you to execute a certain block of code several times. Here is a short introduction on the loops available in Ruby.

- **While loop:** The while loop allows the code to be executed as long as the condition is true. Once it turns false, the execution is stopped, and the program heads over to the next statement.

- **Until loop:** This is the reverse of the while loop. The until loop will keep being executed as long as the condition is false. It will stop when the condition becomes true.

- **For loop:** While Ruby offers a for loop, it is not similar to the for loops available in other programming languages. Instead, the for loop in Ruby functions more like the for each loop in other programming languages. As a result, it will execute the code as long as there are elements to consider in a given expression.

You should be now familiar with the basics of programming in Ruby. Of course, there are still a lot left to go, but these details should help you prepare for the difficult parts.

Conclusion

With the end of this book on programming languages, I hope that it has proven to be useful for you. You should now know about the easiest programming languages for beginners to start with.

Of course, the introduction to programming should have familiarized you with the fundamentals of the activity in general. After all, there are quite a few things that are similar to all languages. One of them is that all languages require you to adopt the mentality of a programmer. Once you do so, you will find programming relatively easier.

As you will have noticed in the book, five languages have been chosen: C, Java, JavaScript, Python and Ruby. These were chosen not only because they are easy to learn but also because they introduce you to the world of programming in a way few other languages can. They are versatile, and you will find it easier to learn other more advanced programming languages.

You should now be familiar with the features of each of the programming languages and know how to write the basic Hello World program for each. You will have also learned some of the basics for all of these languages.

I wish you all the best for your future in programming. With a bit of perseverance and hard work, you will find yourself writing complex code in no time.

Before you jump on your computer, I would like you to post an HONEST REVIEW on Amazon.com in order to improve the quality of the book.

Thank you.

JAVASCRIPT
Learn the Fundamentals of the JavaScript Computer Programming Language

By: Marc Rawen

Table of Contents

Introduction

Getting started in a new programming language is not always so easy. There are many of them that you are able to start with, but some are really complicated to learn, some are a little slow, and others may not be able to do the tasks that you are looking for.

If you are looking for a programming language that is able to work well on websites and gives you some freedom with working on other coding languages, JavaScript is one of the best for you to use. You will find that it is an easy language to learn, being based on English and with the ability to space out the coding so that it looks nice and is easy to read. It also has a lot of speed and the capabilities of working with a variety of browsers and other coding languages so you are able to make this work for any of your website needs.

This guidebook is going to take some time to look at JavaScript and how it works. We will take some time to look at variables, the "if" statements and even the operators that are going to help you to make this code work. This is the perfect guidebook to learn and use when you are first getting started with this programming language and you will be ready to write some of your own codes by the time you are done.

When you are ready to learn a new coding language, or you would like to add another one to your knowledge base, make sure to read through this guidebook and find out how to make JavaScript work for you!

Chapter 1: Getting Started with JavaScript

When it comes to working in a programming language, there are a lot of choices that you are able to make. You can use one that is the best for working on a web page and others will make it easier to make games and other programs that you really want. Coding can be exciting no matter what you want to do, but JavaScript is one of the best and easiest languages to use, especially if you want to add in some extra options for your website. It is easy to work with, uses the same library as Java (which can be helpful if you already know that language), and has all the power and benefits that you can hope for.

There are quite a few reasons why you would consider going with JavaScript as your chosen coding language. While there are many other coding languages that you can use, this one is the easiest to use and the most versatile. And since there are a lot of programmers that will use this code, it is pretty common to find it present in websites and other designing options. Some of the benefits of using JavaScript instead of one of the other programming languages include:

- Execution is on the client side—this means that your speed is going to be faster than on other options. You won't have to worry about bandwidth slowing down the speed so the client will be able to view your information pretty quickly.
- The language is easy—compared to other coding languages, JavaScript is really easy to learn. If you have worked with Java in the past, it is even easier. You will be able to read through it easily and with a big library, creating the code is pretty easy.
- Fast—when JavaScript is in use, you will notice that the speed is really fast. The user will be able to have the code show up on their system in a few seconds, rather than getting impatient with the load time.
- Simple—many of those who are new to coding worry that it is going to be too hard to use. They have looked at some of the other coding languages and think they are too hard to use. But JavaScript is easy to learn and you are going to love how it is easy to work with, even if you don't have any experience with coding in the past.
- Works with web pages—JavaScript is meant to work with web pages. They are usually found in the videos or other add-ons that you want within the page to make it more functional and easier to use.
- Versatility—JavaScript is able to do a lot of the great projects that you want. But if you wish to work on a project that is not covered by JavaScript, you will be able to add it into another coding language and get more done.

Things to remember with JavaScript

While JavaScript is a great programming language that you will be able to learn how to use, there are a few things to remember. First, JavaScript is not a language that is able to create a whole website; you will need to use Java for this. JavaScript can work well with Java to put some add-ons to your program, but you will not be able to create the whole page.

In addition, for the most part, you will put the JavaScript code in the header of the web page. There are some variations that allow you to put this in the body, to have the code in the header and the body, and even to put the code in using an external file to make it safer, but most programmers will leave this code within the header.

You also need to watch out for some of the issues that come with JavaScript. It is not always the best to work with across various browsers. The developers are working to make JavaScript easier to use across a lot of different browsers, but there are some times when this is a challenge. This can be a hassle because coders have to figure out how to make the code they create with JavaScript work across all the platforms and browsers that someone may use in order to bring this code up. Hopefully, this is an issue that JavaScript is able to work out and make a little bit better.

There is just so much that you are going to be able to do when it comes to using JavaScript for your own personal uses. You will be able to read through it quickly because the language is simple, written out well, and the words are in English so you won't have to worry about learning new symbols and signs. It is fast and can provide a lot of benefits and new features that you can't find with other programming languages. And it is also going to be able to work with other coding languages so that it is easy to get everything done that you really want with this language.

Downloading JavaScript

Getting JavaScript started up is pretty simple. You will be able to set this up on any program that you want as long as you bring in the right components so that the code can be written and executed properly. You will need to make sure that you set up the right environment for writing the code. Eclipse is one of the best environments to work with JavaScript because it is set up to work with this coding language and it is really easy to install. Some of the steps that you can take when setting up Eclipse include:

- Go online and look up the link for downloading eclipse. You should check out the latest version that is stable on eclipse and then make sure that you are picking the right kind. For example, if you have a 64-bit computer, you should choose the 64-bit eclipse option. You can find eclipse downloads at https://eclipse.org/downloads
- When the box comes up, click on the elipse.exe in order to open up the file. You can choose which local directory that you would like to use as the workspace.
- You get the choice of choosing or creating a directory on your drive and then can click the OK button to get started.
- When you get to this point, you will need to navigate to File, New, Static Web Project. You then click on the link that will allow you to open the dialogue box that asks you to enter your projects' name.
- Pick what you would like to call the project and then click on the finish button.
- You will notice on the left side of Eclipse, you can expand the directory of the project and on the right, you can click on the "WebContent" folder. You can add an HTML file to your current project. Just go to New and then HTML. This will open up the dialogue box that you can enter a file name for. Click on Finish again and this will add in the HTML file to your current project.

After you are done with signing up for Eclipse and getting it set up, take the time to look through JavaScript library. You are going to find that this is a common programming language and many programmers have used it in the past. This means that there is going to be a big library of terms and syntaxes that you will be able to use to your advantage. These can make it easier to write out the code, find the syntaxes that you need to save time, and can help you to get a good feel for how the language works.

Now that the environment is all set up with JavaScript, you are ready to go. You will just need to open up Eclipse and then open the text box to get your HTML document ready to go. Then simply start to write out the code, using some of the libraries that come with JavaScript as well as some of the fantastic features that come with this language and you are ready to write out your own codes!

In what follows we will frequently refer to a standard HTML file called *JavaScriptCarrier.HTML*.

Type this

```
<!DOCTYPE HTML>
 <HEAD>
<meta charset- "ISO-8859-1">


<TITLE> XYZ </TITLE>


 </HEAD>
 <BODY>



 </BODY>
</HTML>
```

Save it as a template. It will be used again and again.

Chapter 2: Making Codes with JavaScript

If you are a beginner with coding, you may be worried about writing out some of your first codes. You want to be able to write some amazing code, but you are worried that it may be a bit hard or you won't be able to get everything in the right place so that the code can execute in the proper manner. Luckily, many of the modern programming languages are going to make this process a little easier, ensuring that the code stays in the right place instead of moving things around or making it complicated.

When you are working with this coding language, make sure to keep in mind that this is an HTML code, so you need to have the right tags in place so that the code is inserting the right messages on the page. Many of the other coding languages do not have these tags so some beginners and even those who have worked in coding before have trouble remembering this. There are many different types of codes that you will need to use within the code and the one that you choose is going to vary based on the part you are inserting. For example, you can use heading, p (for paragraph), object, script, and more in here based on the command that you want the program to do.

The basic syntax of these tags is simply <script type = "text/javascript"> at the beginning to start out the message or the part that you would like to insert at this part. When all is complete and you want to end that part, you will need to use the symbol </script> and you are good. This is the same for any of the tags that you want to use within your code.

Writing your code

This may seem a little bit challenging to understand at the beginning, so let's go through and try to figure out how it is going to work. Take a look at the code that is listed below and then we will go through and list out each of the parts and what they mean. Then you will be able to go through this information and make some of your own codes with the same kind of steps and parts.

Amend *JavaScriptCarrier.HTML* as follows

```
<!DOCTYPE html>

<html>

<head>

<meta charset- "ISO-8859-1">

<title> My First JavaScript Program </title>

</head>

<body>

        <script language = "javascript"
```

type = "text/javascript">

    document.write("Welcome to JavaScript First Program");

    </script>

</body>

</html>

So now let's take a look at the code and break it up into the different parts so we understand what is being told to the compiler at this point.

Understanding the code

With this block of code, the portion of JavaScript is going to be placed right into the code body. You will need to place this here in some occasions and other times you may want to put a command or something else in place of this to make it work the best for your code. For this part, the code was declared with the right attributes so that once this code is brought up on the web page, you are going to see the words "Welcome to JavaScript First Program" come up on your screen. This is basically going to be known as the output of the code that you just wrote. Keep in mind that you are able to make changes to the wording in this step so that it works for your program.

The white spaces and line spaces

No matter what kind of coding language you are working with, there are often rules that come up concerning the number of line spaces and white spaces that are allowed. The compiler for each of these will read these spaces in different ways. Sometimes the compiler will read these spaces as important so you will need to be really careful about how many returns and spaces you add into the code. Other times the compiler is going to just skip over the white spaces so you are able to add in as many as you would like.

When it comes to using JavaScript, the line breaks and spaces are not as important. The compiler is not going to read through them, so you could write out the code in one straight line if you want; although this is not usually the best way to work because it makes the code really hard to read. Most programmers are going to use a format similar to what we wrote above because it makes the code look a bit nicer and spreads everything out for easier reading.

Using the semicolon

As you may have noticed in the code above, there was a semicolon that came up with the message. When you are done writing out the statement, you should add in the semicolon. It is important to note that this semicolon is not the most important thing in the coding and that the compiler is going to be able to read through the code without it being there, but it is considered good programming form to make sure that the semicolon is in the right place.

Case sensitivity

There are a few programming languages that are going to notice the differences between the uppercase and lowercase letters. They will see the l and the L as different things, while others would read these letters as exactly the same. When you are using JavaScript, the former is true so you must pay attention to which case you are using. If you type in the wrong one when saving the function, it is going to be hard to bring that back up later when you need it.

Comments

Another thing that you may want to use in your code are the comments. These are important because they are going to tell the other programmers what is going on within the code and they can make it easier to explain what you are doing inside the code. The unique thing about these is that you will not see them show up when the code is executed. The compiler will see these comments and choose to just skip over them, allowing these comments to be useful to the people who are using the code, but ensuring that these comments don't come up and interrupt the code when it is being executed.

You can pretty much have as many of these comments in your code as you like. You just need to make sure that you aren't adding in so many that you can't read the actual code and you need to make sure that the write symbols are being used so that the compiler recognizes that the statement is considered a comment and it won't try to read that part. Some of the rules that you should follow when it comes to writing out the right symbols for your code include:

- Single line—if you are writing a block of code that is only going to take up one line, you will need to use the double slash in order to make it show up. Simply placing (//) will show that the comment has started and the interpreter will just skip right over it.
- Multiple lines—sometimes your code is going to take up more than one line. This is allowed in JavaScript as long as you go about it the right way. The best way to write a code that takes up more than one line is to use the </*>...<*/> code around the message that you would like.
- HTML comment--This is the one that is best recognized as an HMTL comment so it can make things easier when you are working on your code, but the choice is yours. To do the HTML comment you would just need the <!—symbol to get it started. You will treat it like a single line of comment so if you need more space, use the other option.

Writing out comments is pretty easy and you will be able to get the hang of using them pretty quickly. If you want to explain what you are doing in the code or what should be placed in that specific spot, you will use a comment. As long as you have the right symbols in front, you are going to be just fine getting this done. Here is a good example of how to work with comments within your code:

```
<!DOCTYPE html>

<html>

<head>

<meta charset = "ISO-8859-1">

<title>JavaScript Comments</title>

</head>

<body>

        <script type = "text/javascript">
```

```
<!—The opening sequence single line comment.
     The closing sequence HTML comment//-->


// This is a single line comment.
/*
*This is a multiple line comment in JavaScript
*/
     </script>
</body>
</html>
```

If you decide to put this code into your program, you will find that nothing will show up. Everything is commented at this point and since the compiler is set up to skip over the comments, you will see nothing come up at all. If you added in a few statements to this, those would be the things that came up on the screen. You can add in as many of these comments as you would like, as demonstrated above, but you will not see them come up on your screen. Mess around with the comments for a bit and you will see how easy they are to create.

Here is a really easy program. Write it and run it.

```
<!DOCTYPE HTML>


<HEAD>
<meta charset = "ISO-8859-1">


<TITLE> XYZ </TITLE>


<script type = "text/javascript >
alert("Hello, world."); //produces little popup box
</script>


</HEAD>


<BODY>
```

The cat sat on the mat.

<hr>

<p>

<button type="button">Press Me Please!</button>

<hr>

<p>

<form>

*Given name:
*

<input type="text" name="givenname">

*
*

*Family name:
*

<input type="text" name="familyname">

</form>

</BODY>

</HTML>

Before we go onto more JavaScript it is worth mentioning that the only JavaScript in this program was

<script type = "text/javascript >

alert("Hello, world."); //produces little popup box

</script>

When the computer saw *<script type = "text/javascript >*, the script tag, it knew that a piece of JavaScript would follow.

The JavaScript command was *alert("Hello, world.");*

When the computer received this command, it carried out the procedure that led to the creation of a little window with "Hello World" in it.

Once that was done the </script> told the computer the JavaScript was finished and it resumed doing HTML leading to a window showing the sentence, ' The cat sat on the mat. ', a button and a form containing some text fields into which information about Given and Family names could be typed.

With regard to comments, it is sensible to put one in even though this is such a simple program.

The alert box is very useful in checking for errors when you do not have a good JavaScript editor.

Standard Math Operations

We will look at these again in Chapter 6 however it is vital that you meet them now.

Open *JavaScriptCarrier.HTML* in your editor

and amend the program so that it now has

```
<hr>
<script type = "text/javascript">
document.write("The sum of 3 and 5 is ");
 document.write(3+5); // program adds 3 and 5
</script>
<hr>
```

between the <body> and </body> tags.

Save the program then run it. If you do you will get this output.

The sum of 3 and 5 is 8

You might notice the two horizontal lines. They are placed there by the HTML tag <hr>. If they were not in what you wrote into the program then the lines would be omitted.

In similar fashion, we could subtract 5 from 3.

We would have to amend the program to

```
<hr>
<script type = "text/javascript">
document.write("Subtracting 5 from 3 gives ");
 document.write(3-5); // program subtracts 5 from 2
</script>
<hr>
```

The output is

Subtracting 5 from 3 gives -2

Similar changes would allow you to multiply and divide.

The correct statements would be

document.write(3*5); for multiply

and

document.write(3/5); for divide.

Outputs should be similar to

Multiplying 5 by 3 gives 15

---

and

Dividing 3 by 5 gives 0.6

A very interesting mathematical operation is **mod**; 17 mod 5 = 2. It is the remainder when we divide 17 by 5. We use % for this in JavaScript. This is a very powerful tool , which you will have to come to grips with.

<script type = "text/javascript">

document.write("The remainder when 17 is divided 5 gives ");

 document.write(17%5); /* program finds the remainder when we divide 17 by 5*/

</script>

Two things to notice:

      (i) You don't put " and " or ' and ' around 3 + 5 if you want a calculation.

      (ii) The semicolon (;) at the end of a statement. JavaScript statements usually work without this, sometimes they don't. That being the case it is good practice to always use it.

Strings

A string is a collection of characters enclosed by " " or ' '. Strings are incredibly important in JavaScript, in fact in most computer languages. You will get to use strings in many practical situations as we proceed but before we go on we need to have a look at some string operations. For anyone using databases, string operations are really important no matter what language you are using.

Open *JavaScriptCarrier.HTML* in your text editor and between the <script type = "text/javascript"> and </script> tags write the following

```
<script type = "text/javascript">
document.write(1+" "+"Ele phant" .charAt(3)+"<br>");
document.write(2+" "+"Ele phant".charAt(4)+"<br>");
document.write(3+" "+"Ele phant".charAt(5)+"<br>");
document.write(4+" "+"Ele "+"ph"+"ant"+"<br>");
document.write(5+" "+"Ele phant".indexOf("p ")+"<br>");
document.write(6+" "+"Ele phant".indexOf("ant")+"<br>");
document.write(7+" "+"Ele phant".replace("ant","ete")+"<br>");
document.write(8+" "+"Ele phant".search("e ph")+"<br>");
document.write(9+" "+"Ele phant".substring(2,7)+"<br>");
document.write(10+" "+"Ele phant".toLowerCase()+"<br>");
document.write(11+" "+"Ele phant".toUpperCase()+"<br>");
</script>
```

then run.

The output should be

1
2 p
3 h
4 Ele phant
5 -1
6 6
7 Ele phete
8 2
9 e pha
10 ele phant
11 ELE PHANT

Running through each line.

1. The letters in a string start from position 0 so the statement "+"Ele phant" .charAt(3)

writes down the character of position 3 which is a blank space.

2. The letters in a string start from position 0 so the statement "+"Ele phant" .charAt(4) writes down the character of position 4 which is p.

3 The letters in a string start from position 0 so the statement "+"Ele phant" .charAt(5) writes down the character of position 4 which is h.

4 The + signs when dealing with strings join them together. The strings in this case are "Ele ", "ph" and "ant". When they are joined together you get Ele phant.

5. This statement instructs the computer to reveal the position of "p ", p followed by a space, in "Ele phant". "p " is not in "Ele phant" so the computer returns -1 which means it couldn't find "p ". Please note the reason it could not find "p " was the space after p.

6. This statement instructs the computer to reveal the position of "ant" in "Ele phant". "ant" is in "Ele phant" at position 6. Remember the first character is at position 0.

7. This statement instructs the computer to replace "ant" in "Ele phant" by "ete'. This is done giving the string "Ele phete".

8. This statement instructs the computer to search for "e ph" in "Ele phant". This is done and is found at position 2.

9. This instruction asks for a substring of the string "Ele phant". This means a set of letters from "Ele phant". The substring asked for starts from the character at position 2 which is e then stops before the character at 7. This is the substring "e pha".

10. This statement instructs the computer to make all characters lower case.

11. This statement instructs the computer to make all characters upper case.

You may be wondering about <br>. If you did not have this the output would go across the page instead of down.
 is an HTML tag which if between two lines causes them to align vertically.

Printing a picture

Make sure you have a picture file of a cat with the suffix .png in the same folder as *JavaScriptCarrier.HTML* then change the code to

<script type = "text/javascript">

*document.write("<img src=' cat.png' alt='cat ' width='20%'>
");/*prints cat picture*/*

</script>

When this is done the output is

or whatever picture you have.

See if you can get a picture with the suffix .jpg and can print it. This is good practice in this important technique.

Two things in the above code may mystify you.

alt='cat ' width='20%'

alt='cat ' tells the computer to write the string 'cat' if it can't find the picture file.

width='20%' tells the computer to produce an image whose size is 20% of the original.

Chapter 3: Variables and How They Work in JavaScript

One of the things that you are able to use in your code writing is variables. Variables will have a value in JavaScript only when you assign it a value so they are basically the characters that are used inside the code. You can add any value to the variable so that the compiler is set to execute what you want on the screen. Basically, there are a few different types of data that you are able to use when doing variables in this code and they include:

- Text—this is basically the data type that is going to be a sequence of words or statements that you would like to have come up on the screen. You can write out any message that you would like, sometimes being a sentence and other times being a longer sequence of text. You can make it something simple like "Thank you for taking the time to visit my page!" A string is a text variable. You can use " instead of "" to enclose a string.

- Numbers—the other type of data that you are able to use with variables are numbers. You can choose to use decimal points or whole numbers in your code based on what you need the code to do.

- Boolean—this is a unique data type that you can use and it basically answers whether the user is giving true or false answers, based on the information that you already put in the code. You can have things come up only if the user answers true or you can work it out so that the program has something come up whether the answer is true or false.

Unlike some of the other online coding languages, you will not see that there is a big difference in JavaScript when you are using integer values or floating point values. You will see that both of these are seen as basically the same when working in JavaScript so you won't have to worry so much about these when you get to work on here.

Working with variables

Using variables is going to be pretty easy when working with JavaScript. The variables are basically going to be the containers for data that you are able to use in the code. You can choose to use these containers and then place your chosen data inside of it. The important part here is that you use the right keyword, the "var" keyword so that the compiler knows that you are working on the variable and so it will bring out the right container that you want to call out. Here is a basic syntax that you are able to look at when it comes to working with variables:

```
<!DOCTYPE html>

<html>

<head>

<meta charset = "ISO-8859-1">
```

```
<title>JavaScript Variables</title>

    <script type = "text/javascript">

    var name = "Appy";

    var age = 21

    var salary = 10000, expenses = 12000;

    alert("Name:" +name + "Age:" + age + "/nSalary:" + salary

                    +"Expenses:" + expenses)

        </script>

        </head>

        <body>

        </body>

    </html>
```

There is a lot of information that is shown within this code. When you take a look at the variable, you will need to do the variable initialization process. Basically, to complete this process, you need to create a brand new variable. You can also do this when you use the variable rather than right at this point. The syntax that is above is going to make it easier to bring up the variables such as name, salary, and age. You will be able to add in as many or as few variables as you would like depending on your needs.

With the code above, there are a few variables that are used and the user will be able to make their pick for the input that they want to put into there. For example, the user can work with the salary variable and they will end up with an answer of 10,000 and if they choose to go with the name variable, they are going to get the answer "appy" So basically when you decide it is time to execute this program onto the screen, the results will be:

Name: Appy
Age: 21
Salary: 10000
Expenses: 12000

What is the scope of my variable?

The next question that you may have with your variable is what its scope is. You need to remember that all the variables are going to have a scope so that they are able to be used. This is the scope that the variable will be based on and without the scope, your program will not be able to find the variable. As the programmer, you will be able to choose from a few scopes that work with the variable, but the global and the local variable. Here are some of the differences that you will see between the two scopes:

- Local variables—when you use the local variable, you are setting up the program so that you are only going to see this variable in the exact location where it is defined. If you set up the parameters to go with that function, then you are pretty much setting up the local scope of the variable that you want to use. You will not be able to see it anywhere else within the program.

- Global variable—for this kind of scope, you will be able to define the variable anywhere within the code and anyone else who uses the program will be able to see it. This can sometimes be nice to use because it helps make sure that others are able to see what is going on and they can be anywhere that they want in the HTML document.

When you are naming the two types of variables, make sure that you are giving them different names to keep from getting confused. If you do name a local and a global variable by the same names, keep in mind that JavaScript is going to see the local variable as the important one so it will bring you the local variable rather than the global variable.

Naming your variable

Another thing that you will need to worry about is how to name your variable. There are a lot of choices in doing this and for the most part, you will be able to name the variable anything that you want without too many issues. With that being said, there are a few things that you should keep in mind. First, make sure that you name the variable something that makes sense and something that will help you to remember what it is. Some of the other rules that you should follow when naming your variable include:

- Do not use the reserved keywords. These are ones that will tell the compiler to do certain tasks so using them as the name of your variable is just going to make a big mess. You can use any other words that you would like outside of these keywords.

- Starting the variable with a number is not allowed. You should use special characters or letters to get started with naming. Basically, you are not allowed to do something like 7children to name the variable, but you could use sevenchildren or _7children.

- You should also remember that the letters inside of your variables are case sensitive. The program is going to see that there is a difference between Boy and boy when you write out the words. Make sure that you remember what you are naming things so that when you try to pull the variable back out, you will be able to get the right one.

Other than these simple rules, you have the freedom to name your variables anything that you want. You can also place objects and other things inside of these variable containers and can pull them out when you need them the most. Learning how to play around with the variables is going to make a big difference in the kind of code you are producing and how it is going to behave when you execute it.

Here are some more examples using variables. In producing these examples we will introduce you to the Math object which allows us to do much mathematics and arrays, a topic of great importance in all computer languages.

Open *JavaScriptCarrier.HTML* in your text editor and replace all content starting with the tag <script type = "text/javascript"> and finishing with </script> with

<script type = "text/javascript">

var surname = prompt('Hello, what is your surname?');/*you enter your surname into a popup. This then becomes the value held by the variable surname*/

document.write(surname);//The variable surname is printed

</script>

Now run the program.

You should see

Followed by a screen showing the name you entered. Say you entered Simons then you'd get

---

Simons

On receiving the line *var surname = prompt('Hello, what is your surname?');*

The computer will put whatever you enter into a piece of memory labeled **surname**. Whenever the word **surname** is encountered then the name entered will come forward. What has just been done is creating a *string* variable called surname.

In the previous example involving strings

<script type = "text/javascript">

document.write(1+" "+"Ele phant" .charAt(3)+"<br>");

...

...

...

document.write(11+" "+"Ele phant".toUpperCase()+"<br>");

</script>

we could have created a variable called **str**. The code would be

```
<script type = "text/javascript">


var str = "Ele phant";


document.write(1+" "+str .charAt(3)+"<br>");

...

...

...

document.write(11+" "+str.toUpperCase()+"<br>");

</script>
```

 Much time would have been saved.

In the same way, as you create string variables which are strings you can create variables which are different types of number.

For example var num = 9; creates an integer variable **num** with the value 9.

var **numba** = 6.75 creates a real number variable with the value 6.75.

Math Object

For those of you familiar with mathematics JavaScript has a built in method of getting many mathematical functions you are familiar with.

Suppose you want random numbers from 0 to 1 then you include

Math.random(). Here is how you might do this.

```
<script type = "text/javascript">

var num = Math.random() ;/*creates a number variable between the values of 0 and 1*/

alert(num);//brings up popup with num displayed

</script>
```

When running you would get the output of little window like this.

0.9340200062313243

OK

Your number would almost certainly differ but you would get a little window with some decimal between 0 and 1.

What is happening is that the Math object creates a random number between 0 and 1 which is assigned to the variable **num.**

The alert procedure then displays **num.**

Suppose you wanted a random integer between 0 and 10. If you want to try this yourself without reading on then do so.

One way to do it is shown.

<script type = "text/javascript">

var num = Math.round(10*Math.random()) ; ;/*creates an integer variable between the values of 0 and 10*/

alert(num););//brings up popup with num displayed

</script>

The output is

4

OK

Pressing OK then refreshing the page gives different integers between 0 and 10.

What is happening is that the Math object creates a random number between 0 and 1 which is multiplied by 10 then Math.round() rounds it off and this is assigned to the variable **num.**

The alert procedure then displays **num.**

There are many such useful functions available through the Math object.

Try this.

<script type = "text/javascript">

var num = Math.PI;//assigns the number ππ to the variable num

alert(num););//brings up popup with num displayed

</script>

The output is

3.141592653589793

OK

What is happening is that the Math object creates the number Pi, or π, which is assigned to the variable **num**.

The alert procedure then displays **num.**

This is incredibly useful if you need to find the circumference or area of a circle. You will see this later.

It is worth mentioning that the Math object is a pre-built object. The term object has great importance in computing and a topic we will cover in much greater depth in Chapter 6.

Arrays

The next topic in this chapter is another one of extraordinary importance. We create a new thing called an array to hold a set of values.

Let us take a really simple example.

<script type = "text/javascript">

var numHold = [5,9,-7];/*creates an array numHold where numHold[0] = 5, numHold[1] = 9, numHold[2] = -7*/

var num = Math.round(2*Math.random());//randomly creates 0, 1, 2 *alert(numHold[num]);/*brings up popup with 5,9 or -7 depending on which of 0,1 or 2 is selected*/*

</script>

If you run this program you will get a succession of little windows showing one of 5, 9 or -7.

The program first creates a new array then puts 5, 9 and -7 into the places numHold[0], numHold[1] and numHold[2].

var num = Math.round(2*Math.random()) creates either 0,1 or 2.

Alert shows what is in whichever of numHold[0], numHold[1] and numHold[2] gets chosen.

One point that needs emphasizing is that if you have an array Ar then it always starts from 0, the first in the list within Ar is Ar[0]. You need to take this into account.

Let's take this a step further.

Try this

<script type = "text/javascript">

var months =
["January","February","March","April","May","June","July","August","September","October","November","December"];

var num = Math.round(11*Math.random());

alert(months[num]);

</script>

This program if you get it running right will give you a succession of little windows with one month shown.

Chapter 4: Loops and Functions in JavaScript

Suppose you wanted to print the word 'Cat' 5 times going down the page.

```
<script type = "text/javascript">
document.write( "Cat"+"<br>");
document.write( "Cat"+"<br>");
document.write( "Cat"+"<br>");
document.write( "Cat"+"<br>");
document.write( "Cat"+"<br>"); //Cat printed 5 times
</script>
```

will do this.

Loops

The above program is very simple but its writing needs improvement. Suppose the task was to write Cat down the page 50 times. It would be very inefficient to write out *document.write("Cat"+"<br>");* fifty times. Fortunately, there are ways in which this can be done. The first way is using what is called a **for** loop.

Type the following piece of code into *JavaScriptCarrier.HTML.*

```
<script type = "text/javascript">
for (i = 1;i<51;i++)//This will print CAT 50 times going down the page
{document.write( "Cat"+"<br>"); }
</script>
```

Part of the output is shown below

Cat
Cat
Cat
Cat
Cat
Cat
Cat
Cat

Note that there is now a comment //*This will print CAT 50 times going down the page.*

There are other loops. One of the most useful is the **while** loop. To see how this works we will create a **while** loop to do what the previous loop did.

Type the following piece of code into *JavaScriptCarrier.HTML.*

```
<script type = "text/javascript">
/* 50 printings of Cat down page using the while loop*/
var count = 1; // This variable counts the number of printings
while (count< 51)
{
document.write( "Cat"+"<br>");
count++; //this increases count by 1 each time a loop is completed
}
</script>
```

The output is once again.

Cat
Cat
Cat
Cat
Cat
Cat
Cat
Cat

There are a couple of other loops but they are not really necessary. You can find out more about them by using Google.

You may wonder if there is any preference between **for** and **while**. There actually isn't and a clever programmer could happily use either however for most people **for** is good for a situation where you have a definite start and finish. **while** is useful for where you are not sure where the finish is.

Let us take a situation where **for** would be better.

If we had an array of 100 names and wanted to print the 20th name to the 30th then try this.

<script type = "text/javascript">

/* This program prints all names in the list from the 20th to the 30th*/

var nam = ["Adam","Alfred","Andy","Axe","Ben","Briar","Bob","Betty","Bollinger", "Byron","Cam","Cathie","Amy","Cindy","Charles","Chas", "Chan","Chen","Chin"," Chong","Dave","Don","Dilworth","Drue","Dudley","Doberman","Dan","Den","Exeter","Dong","Evans","Evan","Emma","PooBar","Fosdick","Fuamano","Frost","Grimes","Gent"," Grunge","Harry","Henry","Hopa","Hupa","Hurring","Heeney","Hemi","Hemmings","Hope","Hong","Innes","Ira","Ivan","Imogen","Ivy","Jon","John","Jane","Jhani","Juliet","Kristina", "Katrina","Kathy", "Kate","Kitty","Lewis", "Louis","Lupe","Linda","Lulu","Leonie","Mervyn","Mary","Marea","Marama","Moira"," Nancy","Nellie","Nulla","Needham","Oprah","Otis","Piere","Ramesh","Opus","Opo","Papa","Paul","Prince","Peroy","Piutus","Bull", Hoskin","Karen", "Sewell","Lillian", "Zulu","Wong","Willy","Wiremu"];//These are the names

for (i = 19;i<30;i++)//This will print names 20-30 down the page

{document.write(nam[i]+"<br>"); }

</script>

The output is

Chong
Dave
Don
Dilworth
Drue
Dudley
Doberman
Dan
Den
Exeter
Dong

A couple of points need to be raised.

(i) Remember that an array always starts from 0 so the 20th will be number 19 and the 30th will be number 29.

(ii) I have called the array containing the names *nam*. I could have called it just about anything but in selecting variable names give the variables names, which are close to what they represent. It is an interesting fact that you have to be careful about choosing names for variables, as some are what are called *reserved words*, which means they have a special meaning within a program. If you called the array *name* you will get funny results, as name is a reserved word.

Now for a program that definitely is easier with **while**.

Suppose you wanted to print all names in the array of names until you encountered one with more than 6 letters.

The number of characters in a string *str* is *str.length*.

Here is a program which will do this:

<script type = "text/javascript">

/* This program prints all names in the list until you get one with more than 6 letters*/

var count =0;//This counts the number of loops.

var nam = ["Adam","Alfred","Andy","Axe","Ben","Briar","Bob","Betty","Bollinger", "Byron","Cam","Cathie","Amy","Cindy","Charles","Chas", "Chan","Chen","Chin","Chong","Dave","Don","Dilworth","Drue","Dudley","Doberman","Dan","Den","Exeter","Dong","Evans","Evan","Emma","PooBar","Fosdick","Fuamano","Frost","Grimes","Gent","Grunge","Harry","Henry","Hopa","Hupa","Hurring","Heeney","Hemi","Hemmings","Hope","Hong","Innes","Ira","Ivan","Imogen","Ivy","Jon","John","Jane","Jhani","Juliet","Kristina", "Katrina","Kathy", "Kate","Kitty","Lewis",
"Louis","Lupe","Linda","Lulu","Leonie","Mervyn","Mary","Marea","Marama","Moira","Nancy","Nellie","Nulla","Needham","Oprah","Otis","Piere","Ramesh","Opus","Opo","Papa","Paul","Prince","Percy","Pratus","Bali","Hoskin","Karen", "Sewell","Lillian",
"Zulu","Wong","Willy","Wiremu"];//These are the names

var howManyLetters = nam[count].length ;/*This variable will hold the number of letters in a name as we go through the loop. It starts with the length of the first member of nam*/

while (howManyLetters<7)//This will print required names down the page

    {

    document.write(nam[count]+"<br>");

    count++; //Each time we do a loop count increases by 1

howManyLetters = nam[count].length;//each time we increase count we make howManyLetters the length of the next member of nam

}

</script>

The output is shown below

Adam
Alfred
Andy
Axe
Ben
Briar
Bob
Betty

Functions

All computer languages, with the possible exception of the most simple use functions. A function is a block of code that does something or returns some value. In JavaScript we use functions. They also provide a stepping stone into the world of object-oriented programming which is very important nowadays.

Consider the last program, which took the list of names and printed those whose length was less than 7. A function could be made out of this. Here's how.

In the head or some other part of the file *JavaScriptCarrier.HTML*. type

<script type = "text/javascript">

function shortNames()

{

/ This program prints all names in the list until you get one with more than 6 letters*/*

var count =0;//This counts the number of loops.

var nam = ["Adam","Alfred","Andy","Axe","Ben","Briar","Bob","Betty","Bollinger", "Byron","Cam","Cathie","Amy","Cindy","Charles","Chas", "Chan","Chen","Chin","Chong","Dave","Don","Dilworth","Drue","Dudley","Doberman","Dan","Den","Exeter","Dong","Evans","Evan","Emma","PooBar","Fosdick","Fuamano","Frost","Grimes","Gent","Grunge","Harry","Henry","Hopa","Hupa","Hurring","Heeney","Hemi","Hemmings","Hope","Hong","Innes","Ira","Ivan","Imogen","Ivy","Jon","John","Jane","Jhani","Juliet","Kristina", "Katrina","Kathy", "Kate","Kitty","Lewis",
"Louis","Lupe","Linda","Lulu","Leonie","Mervyn","Mary","Marea","Marama","Moira","Nancy","Nellie","Nulla","Needham","Oprah","Otis","Piere","Ramesh","Opus","Opo","Pap

a","Paul","Prince","Percy","Pratus","Bali","Hoskin","Karen", "Sewell","Lillian",
"Zulu","Wong","Willy","Wiremu"];//These are the names

var howManyLetters = nam[count].length ;/*This variable will hold the number of letters in a name as we go through the loop. It starts with the length of the first member of nam*/

while (howManyLetters<7) //This will print required names down the page

{

document.write(nam[count]+"<br>");

count++; //Each time we do a loop count increases by 1

howManyLetters = nam[count].length;

}

}//end of function shortNames()

</script>

Now somewhere in the body type <script type = "text/javascript"> shortNames(); </script>.

If *JavaScriptCarrier.HTML* has opened then the function *shortNames()* operates and we get the same output as before.

This may seem a fairly useless demonstration so we will make it a bit more useful by giving what is called a *parameter*.

Replace the declaration of shortNames() with shortNames(n) in the following way.

<script type = "text/javascript">

function shortNames(n)

{

/* This program prints all names in the list until you get one with more than 6 letters*/

this.n = n;//this.n ensures that the program understands that any reference to n is to this n and not some other n

var count =0;//This counts the number of loops.

var nam = ["Adam","Alfred","Andy","Axe","Ben","Briar","Bob","Betty","Bollinger", "By-

ron","Cam","Cathie","Amy","Cindy","Charles","Chas", "Chan","Chen","Chin","
Chong","Dave","Don","Dilworth","Drue","Dudley","Doberman","Dan","Den","Exeter","D
ong","Evans","Evan","Emma","PooBar","Fosdick","Fuamano","Frost","Grimes","Gent","
Grunge","Harry","Henry","Hopa","Hupa","Hurring","Heeney","Hemi","Hemmings","Ho
pe","Hong","Innes","Ira","Ivan","Imogen","Ivy","Jon","John","Jane","Jhani","Juliet","Kri
stina", "Katrina","Kathy", "Kate","Kitty","Lewis",
"Louis","Lupe","Linda","Lulu","Leonie","Mervyn","Mary","Marea","Marama","Moira","
Nancy","Nellie","Nulla","Needham","Oprah","Otis","Piere","Ramesh","Opus","Opo","Pap
a","Paul","Prince","Percy","Pratus","Bali","Hoskin","Karen", "Sewell","Lillian",
"Zulu","Wong","Willy","Wiremu"];//These are the names

var howManyLetters = nam[count].length;/*This variable will hold the number of letters
in a name as we go through the loop.*/

while (howManyLetters<n) //This will print required names down the page

{

document.write(nam[count]+"<br>");

count++; //Each time we do a loop count increases by 1

howManyLetters = nam[count].length;//howMany letters becomes length of next name

}

}//end of function shortNames(n)

</script>

The section which used to be <script type = "text/javascript"> shortNames(); </script>
is replaced by

<script type = "text/javascript">

var n = prompt("What number of letters must the word not have?");// we enter n

shortNames(n);

</script>

The reader must think we are hypocritical using n as the name of a variable. It would actually be preferable to use some more descriptive name such as maxLetter. The important point was to demonstrate the use of n as the parameter.

The .js file

The final part of this chapter is to demonstrate something called a JavaScript file. Frequently, you will need to use the same code again and again over possibly hundreds of web pages. Here is how you could do this far more efficiently than writing the code again and again.

With your text editor write all your functions in a totally separate file from the HTML files. Call that file any name you wish but avoid any reserved words.

To illustrate how this works, I am putting my *shortNames(n)* function in a file called *lib.js*. What I must do now is to ensure that *lib.js* is in the same folder as my HTML file. I cannot emphasize how important this is. If you don't want your program to work then have the *.js* and *.HTML* files in different folders

The HTML is now the following

<!DOCTYPE HTML>

<HEAD>

<meta charset = "ISO-8859-1">

<TITLE> ABC </TITLE>

<script src="lib.js"></script>

</HEAD>

<BODY>

<hr>

<script type = "text/javascript"> var n = prompt("What number of letters must the word not have?");//we enter n

shortNames(n);

</script>

<hr>

</BODY>

</HTML>

The crucial line is *<script src="lib.js"></script>*

This tells JavaScript that it should look in the source file (src) *lib.js* for functions if they are not in the HTML file.

This technique of using source files is a very powerful and useful technique and saves a huge amount of work.

Chapter 5: Can My Coding Make Decisions?

There are times when you will want to teach the computer program to make some decisions for you. You can set up the program to accept answers from the user, but depending on the answer, you may want different things to happen. For example, if you are doing a program that asks what 2 +2 equals, you will want to make sure that you have different things occur when the user inputs 4 or another number. It wouldn't make much sense to have the same statement, such as "Congratulations, you got the right answer!" if the user put in the number 5.

There are ways that you will be able to teach the program to make decisions based on the criteria that you set. You will need to tell the program what answer you accept and then can tell it what it should do when the answer is correct and what it should do if the user puts in the incorrect answer. The statements that we are going to talk about in this chapter will give you some options. You could set it up so that it tells the user that they are right only when they put in the correct answer and then the program will end, or you can pick a more complicated method, which we will discuss in this chapter as well, and have one answer come up when they are correct and another option come up when they are wrong.

These kinds of statements are known as conditional statements and there are actually a few different kinds that you are able to use within your code. As discussed, some are only going to respond when the user puts in the right answer and others are going to respond in different ways based on whether the user is right or wrong. You can also do variations where three or more statements will come up based on the answer that the user gives, such as if you want a different answer to come up for a variety of age groups rather than just two options.

The different conditional statements that you can choose from that will help the program decide what you want it to do based on the conditions you give and the information that the user puts in includes:

- If statements
- If...else statement
- If...else if statements
- Switch case statements

If statements

Let's take a look at how the if statements will work. These are the most basic of the conditional statements you will work with and it is a good one to get started with when learning how to use these kinds of statements. They are going to work ad the conditions that you are setting and determine if the user input is considered true based on these conditions. If the code determines that the information is true within the conditions you set, the program will go ahead and execute the message or the statement that you placed inside of it. On the other hand, when using the if statement, when the user puts in an input that is considered false based on the conditions that you set, the program will just end or move on to the other block of code that you set up, without taking the time to put out a statement.

A good example of this is working with ages. Say you are setting up a program that wants to encourage people to vote and provide them with their polling area. But the user has to be 18 to vote. You would be able to use the "if" statement in order to set up the conditions so that the true answers would need to have a number that is 18 or above to be true. With this code, if the user put in the answer 21, they would be true and would instigate the statement that you put in, such as "Congratulations, you can vote! Here are the details of your local polling place!" On the other hand, if they put in their age as 16, the program would see that this is false and then the program would end.

When you are ready to get a feel for how the if statements work, take some time to try out this syntax.

```
<!DOCTYPE html>

<html>

<head>

<meta charset = "ISO-8859-1">

<title>Basic IF Statement</title>

</head>

<body>

        <script type = "text/javascript">

        var salary = 10000;

        var expenses = 12000;

        if(expenses > salar){

        document.write("<b>Please either start earning more or spend less!</b>"):

        }

        </script>

            <p>We are inside the body section...</p>

        </body>

        </html>
```

Give this code a try and see how it is going to turn out. You can try out a few different answers to see what happens when you enter a true value and what happens when you enter a value that the program sees as false. You can always change up the numbers within the code as well and using the < or > sign can be helpful if you want to get a range of numbers or ages.

The if...else statement

With the example that we looked at above, there is only a right answer. If the user puts in an answer that fits as right within the code, your program will give them a statement or message that you inserted into the code. But if the user puts in a number that is considered false by the program, the program will just end on them.

This is something that you usually don't want to happen. Who wants their program to just end without a message or something that tells the user why the answer is wrong or gives them directions? For example, if the user put in that they are 16 and you want the number to be 18 or above for being able to vote, you may want to have a statement like "You are not eligible to vote, try next election." Rather than just having the program end, you want to have something show up on the screen.

This is where the if...else statement is going to come into play. It allows you to have one message that comes up if the input of the user is true based on your conditions and then another statement will come up if the answer the program is given is considered false. This can make the program more advanced and easier to make a more complex program. You often want to have something come up regardless of the answer that the user gives.

You are able to have as many of the if...else statements come up as you would like so you aren't stuck with just one true and one false. For example, perhaps you want to divide up age groups into four different categories. You could have a group o 0 to 2, 3 to 5, 6 to 8, and 9 to 10. The user would be able to input the age of their child in order to get the information that you have available and each age they pick will provide them with the statement that you put into the program and then it will direct them to the place that they want. While most beginners are going to start with just two or three of these if...else statements, you can technically have as many as you would like if you use the right syntax in the process.

The syntax for the if...else statements is simple to get started with. Take a look at this syntax below and give it a try on your compiler to see how it all comes together:

<!DOCTYPE html>

<html>

<head>

<meta charset = "ISO-8859-1">

<title>If Else Statement</title>

```
</head>

<body>

        <script type = "text/javascript">

        var salary = 12000;

        var expenses = 10000;

        if(expenses > salary){

        document.write("<b>Please either start earning more or spend less!</b>"):

        }

        else {

                document.write("<b>You have enough money to spend!</b>");

        </script>

                <p>We are inside the body section...</p>

        </body>

        </html>
```

With this example, you are only using one of the if...else statements, but you could always add in some more based on what you would like to do with the program. You can also change up the statements and the messages that come up on the screen while you are working on your code. This allows you to have some more freedom when it is time to create the code and you can have a variety of options, statements, and more come up based on the input that your user gives to you.

These are the two basic types of conditional statements that you should learn how to use when working in JavaScript. There are other options that will help you to give your user a choice, such as using the ordering game so that they can pick which number they want to do based on the food or menu item that is beside it. You can separate out ages to show what each one is able to do. There is just so much that you are able to do with these conditional statements and this can really make it easier to expand your code and make some amazing things happen even as a beginner.

Make sure to take some time to learn how to make some of these conditional statements so that you can get the results that you are looking for when writing out your code. There are many options that you will want to have come up based on the answers that the user is able to give and what you ultimately want the code to be able to do. With some practice, the if and the if...else statements are going to help you to really make a big difference in your own code.

We now give some more examples of this type programming called *conditional programming*. We will also have a look at the logic operators AND(&&), OR(||) and NOT(!). It is very pertinent to see how equality and inequality are written in JavaScript programs

We will continue to refer to a standard HTML file called *JavaScriptCarrier.HTML* but we are going to put all our functions in the JavaScript file we created called *lib.js*.

JavaScriptCarrier.HTML should be as below

<!DOCTYPE HTML>

<HEAD>
<meta charset = "ISO-8859-1">
<TITLE> ABC </TITLE>

<script src="lib.js"></script>

</HEAD>

<BODY>

<script type = "text/javascript">
Code goes here using functions stored on lib.js
</script>

</BODY>

</HTML>

The line *<TITLE> ABC </TITLE>* is optional. If you like you can totally delete this

We start with something very simple.

Suppose you randomly generated 0 or 1. If 0 was generated then an alert with 'Cat' would come up. If 1 was generated then the output would be an alert with 'Dog'

Create a new function *randomCatDog(n) in lib.js.*

The initial step is to write what is below.

function randomCatDog(n)

{

}

This is the randomCatDog function. As there is nothing between the curly brackets the function does nothing. It is only when we put some JavaScript instructions in between the curly braces that randomCatDog(n) will do something. Notice that there is a parameter n.

In JavaScript, the conditional operators are **if** and **if/else**. We will show the use of both, however, this example needs **if/else**.

Now make sure *randomCatDog(n)* is as below.

function randomCatDog(n)

{

this.n = n;// inform the program that n refers to the parameter

if (n ==0)

    {

   alert("Cat");

    }

else

    {

   alert("Dog");

    }

}//end of randCatDog(n)

Note the use of == when equals is a comparison. This is vitally important.

Under no circumstances write (n = 0); if you do the program thinks you are assigning the value 0 to n. So remember == for comparisons and = for assignments.

In the body of *JavaScriptCarrier.HTML* write

<script type = "text/javascript">

var n = Math.round(Math.random());//Randomly creates either 1 or 0

randomCatDog(n);

</script>

Note my use of the name *randomCatDog()* for the function. Functions like variables should have a good relation to their purpose.

There is another version of **if/else** which is **if/else if/else** which is used when there are more than 2 choices.

Suppose you generated randomly the numbers 0, 1, 2, 3, 4 and 5. If you generated 0 or 1 you got 'Cat', 2 or 3 gave 'Dog' and 4, 5 gave 'Hog'

Here is how you could do it.

function randomCatDogHog(n)

{

this.n = n;// inform the program that n refers to the parameter n

if (n <2)

    {

    alert("Cat");//the alert says "Cat" if 0 or 1 are generated

    }

else if (n<5)

    {

    alert("Dog"); the alert says "Dog" if 2 or 3 are generated

    }

else

    {

    alert("Hog"); the alert says "Hog" if 4 or 5 are generated

    }

}//end of randCatDogHog(n)

The code in the body of *JavaScriptCarrier.HTML* would be

<script type = "text/javascript">

var n = Math.round(5*Math.random());//Randomly creates 0,1,......5

randomCatDogHog(n);

</script>

Note the use of < as a comparison operator. This operator means *less than*, there is also > for *greater than*, >= for *greater than or equal* and <= for *less than or equal*.

There are three choices in the program above and you could have as many *else if* as you wish as you increase the number of choices. You must always finish with *else*.

There is also a *switch* operator that does this as well but we won't consider it. If you are interested do a Google search for it.

Now let's write a program which uses **if** but does not require **if/else** or **if/else if/else**.

Suppose you had the array *["marbles","cards","counters","tickets","clips","sweets", "cats", "frogs"]*

and wanted to print all words with at least 6 letters.

Here is the code that will do it.

In *lib.js* type the following empty function.

function typeItems(n)

{

}

Now fill it as follows:

```
function typeItems(n)
{
this.n = n;//ensures function uses n in parameter


var things = ["marbles","cards","counters","tickets","clips","sweets", "cats", "frogs"];//
array of things


for(i=0;i<things.length;i++)//things.length is the number of elements in things. In this
case it is 8
    {

        if (things[i].length >= n)//if the number of letters in things[i] is at least n then
        things[i] is printed.
            {
            document.write(things[i]+"<br>");//instruction to print things[i]
            }


    }
}//end of function typeItems(n)
```

Now type the following code into the body of *JavaScriptCarrier.HTML*

```
<script type = "text/javascript">
var n = 6;// We want to print elements in the array which have at least six letters
typeItems(n);
</script>
```

Open *JavaScriptCarrier.HTML* and your output should be

marbles

counters

tickets

sweets

Conditional Operators

The next topic is of fundamental importance. It is easy for those who are quite good at mathematics or logic however others sometimes find it challenging.

AND

You use AND between two conditions if they both have to be true. In JavaScript AND is represented by *&&*.

Let us carry out a very simple example. Suppose the computer randomly generates 1 or 0 then picks one of the letters A or B.

If 1 AND B are picked an alert goes up saying "Congratulations, you picked 1 and B" else an alert goes up saying "Sorry you need 1 and B"

Type this into *lib.js*.

function randomNumLetter()

{

var num = Math.round(Math.random());//selects 0 or 1 randomly

var letterNum = Math.round(Math.random());//selects 0 or 1 randomly

var let = "A";

if (letterNum==1){let = "B";}//the letter is A for letterNum being 0 and B otherwise.

If ((num ==1)&&(let=="B")) //both 1 and B have to be generated

*   {alert("Congratulations, you picked 1 and B")}*

else

*   { alert("Sorry, you need 1 and B")}*

}//end of function randomNumLetter()

Now type the following code into the body of *JavaScriptCarrier.HTML*

```
<script type = "text/javascript">
randomNumLetter();
</script>
```

Open *JavaScriptCarrier.HTML* in your favorite browser to see this.

OR

You use OR between two conditions if one or both of them are true. In JavaScript OR is represented by ||.

To demonstrate it we will use the function *typeItems(n)* used before and modify it so that it prints items of length *m* or *n*.

Here is the function, which should be typed into *lib.js*.

```
function typeItems1(m,n)

{

this.m = m;//ensures function uses m in parameter

this.n = n;//ensures function uses n in parameter


var things = ["marbles","cards","counters","tickets","clips","sweets", "cats", "frogs"];//array of things


for(i=0;i<things.length;i++)//things.length is the number of elements in things. In this case it is 8

    {


        if ((things[i].length == m)|| (things[i].length == n))//if the number of letters in things[i] is m or n then things[i] is printed.

            {

            document.write(things[i]+"<br>");//instruction to print things[i]

            }
```

```
    }
}//end of function typeItems1(m,n)
```

Now type the following code into the body of *JavaScriptCarrier.HTML*

```
<script type = "text/javascript">
var m = 4;// We want to print elements in the array which have four letters
var n = 5;// We want to print elements in the array which have five letters
typeItems1(m,n);
</script>
```

After opening *JavaScriptCarrier.HTML* in your favorite browser the output is

cards
clips
cats
frogs

NOT

You use in front of a condition so that the procedure occurs when the condition is not fulfilled. In JavaScript NOT is represented by !

To demonstrate it, we will use the function typeItems(n) used before and modify it so that it prints items of length whose length is not at least *n*.

Here is the function that should be typed up in lib.js

```
function typeItems2(n)

{

this.n = n;//ensures function uses n in parameter


var things = ["marbles","cards","counters","tickets","clips","sweets", "cats", "frogs"];//
array of things
```

for(i=0;i<things.length;i++)//things.length is the number of elements in things. In this case it is 8

> *{*

>> *if (!(things[i].length >= n))//if the number of letters in things[i] is NOT at least n then things[i] is printed.*

>>> *{*

>>> *document.write(things[i]+"<br>");//instruction to print things[i]*

>>> *}*

> *}*

}//end of function typeItems2(n)

Now type the following code into the body of *JavaScriptCarrier.HTML*

<script type = "text/javascript">

var n = 6;// We want to print elements in the array which do NOT have at least six letters

typeItems2(n);

</script>

After opening *JavaScriptCarrier.HTML* in your favorite browser the output is

cards
clips
cats
frogs

As you can see the words that do not have at least 6 letters have been printed.

Chapter 6: The Importance of Learning about Objects in JavaScript

JavaScript, as well as many of the other modern coding languages, are considered an object-oriented programming language. This makes it easier for the coder to work inside since some of the bugs that were in the older versions of coding languages have been cleaned up a little bit over time. But since this one is based off real life objects, you need to make sure that you are using the objects in the proper way so that the compiler is able to execute the codes that you are placing inside the program.

In these kinds of languages, the objects are basically going to be parts of the program that you are using and each of the objects can have certain attributes to help define them. These are sometimes going to include the function of your object and others are going to include the method. An easier way to think about these objects is to think about how they look, feel, and act. Let's take some time to look at these objects and learn how you will be able to place them into your code with JavaScript to get the best results.

Learning about the different properties of your objects

There is going to be some diversity when you are making properties that will come off the objects. You get some freedom when choosing the data types that will go into the objects including numbers, strings, and Boolean values. There are also some times when the object will be a bit more abstract compared to the other data types. You will find that the properties of your objects though are going to be attached to the variables that you used when creating the object.

Keep in mind that when you create an object, they are going to be global variables. This basically means that when you create a new object, you will be able to see it throughout the whole page, not just in the location where you originally created them. This is going to happen any time that you place the objects into the computer and into the code properly. Having the object being a global variable is going to make it easier for the coder to find what they want when searching the code for the object.

Here is a good sample of what you will need to do when trying to create objects through your code:

```
<!DOCTYPE html>
<html>
<head>
<meta charset = "ISO-8859-1">
<title>Objects Example </title>
        <script type = "text/javascript">
                objectName.objectProperty = propertyValue;
                        var str = document.title;
        </script>
</head>
<body>
```

```
</body>
</html>
```

When you put this syntax into the compiler, you will see that you have already gone through the process of giving the right variable to the different places within the code. These are some of the locations that you are going to want to use along with the objects when your code is executed.

The relationship between the objects and their methods

When we talk about the methods of an object, we are basically going to be talking about the functions of those objects, the functions that you must use in order to manipulate or execute the object so that they behave the way that you want within the code. The function is going to run in a different way compared to the method because the function is able to work both as a standalone and as a statement while your method is always going to be tied to a certain keyword within the code and can only run in the way that this particular keyword allows it.

In this case, the method is going to be used in your syntax to display the object contents into the HTML page. They will often use this to help write out the parameters that you would like to have on your object method as well as some of the various operations that you would want to use in the code. Or you can even choose to use the write() method so that you can pass this text string on to the page, making it easier for the user to see this statement or this string on the screen when the program is executed.

How to make the operator show up on the page

This section is going to spend some time looking at your new operator because it is going to be one of the most important parts of the code when you get started. This new operator is basically the one that you will use in order to create an instance in the object. If you are trying to create this particular object in JavaScript, you need to make sure that the new operator that you created is going to be placed in the code correctly so that it will execute properly and do the work that it needs.

The constructor method is one of your tools that you need to learn when working with a new operator. You must make sure that the right function is being used in order to get it to work the right way. For this constructor method to work properly, you have a choice of three functions to use including data(), object(), and array(). Let's look at how this is going to work within your code and how you can write out the syntax:

```
<!DOCTYPE.html>
<html>
<head>
<meta charset = "ISO-8859-1">
<title>The New Operator</title>
<script type = "text/javascript">
       var student = new object()
       var languages = new array
("JavaScript", "Pascal", "Python");
       var day = new Date("August 24, 1989");
              alert (day);
</script>
```

```
</head>
<body>
</body>
</html>
```

Take a moment to place this into your JavaScript interpreter to see what is going to come up. If you did this properly and have it executed into the HTML program, you will see that an alert box will come up. This box will state the date that you place here as well as the time and all the additional information that you have put into the code above. You will be able to make some changes to what comes up in the alert box as you need, but this is a great way to get started and to see how the objects can be placed within the code.

As you can see, working with objects will be pretty simple in JavaScript and they can give you a lot of freedom in terms of the code that you are creating. You don't need to make things complicated, though. The syntax that is given above is basically going to allow you to put the time and date into the system and get an alert box. You can change it how you would like it to come up and which objects are going to be shown, but it is basically going to work the same each time you do this process.

If you did not follow this then examine the following piece of code.

```
<script type = "text/javascript">
        var circle = {radius:1 , area:function() { var r = this.radius;  var a = Math.PI*r*r;
return a; } };



                alert (circle.radius); //displays radius when it is 1
                circle.radius = 2;     //changes radius to 2
        alert (circle.radius); // displays radius when it is 2
        alert(circle.area());// shows circle's area when radius is 2.

</script>
```

This code creates a circle object with one property its *radius* which is 1 and one inbuilt function a method *area()* which generates its area.

The first alert shows the circle's radius when it is 1.

circle.radius = 2; changes radius to 2.

This is displayed by the second alert finally the method is called and the area calculated then displayed by an alert.

As an exercise see if you can construct a method which computes the circumference. See if you can adjust the code so the radius is 3.

Chapter 7: Learning About the Operators

The operators are going to be some of the easiest, and yet the most important, parts of the code that you are going to need to help tell the code what you want to get done. There are a variety of purposes for using the operator and depending on how you list it within the code, it will have different meanings to get things done. There are a lot of neat things that you are able to do with your operators so let's take a look at the different kinds of operators that are recognized in JavaScript and how you will be able to use the signs to get things done in this coding language.

Using your arithmetic operators

The first operator type that we will look at is the arithmetic operator. As the name suggests, this is basically the type that you are going to use when you want the compiler to do some kind of arithmetic function, whether we are talking about addition, subtraction, multiplication, or division. There are many programs that would use these kinds of operators so they are good ones to learn how to use. Some of the arithmetic operators that you should use in your code include:

- (+)—this is the addition operator and it is going to tell the code to add together two operands such as X + Y
- (-)—this is the subtraction operator and it is used in your code to subtract the second of your operands from the first one such as X − Y
- (*)—this one will be used as the multiplication operator and can be used in order to multiply two operands together such as X * Y.
- (/)—this is the division operator and it will be used in your code in order to divide the two operands such as X / Y
- (%)—this is the modulus which is the operator that will output the remainder of the integer division. You will show this by X % Y
- (++) this is the increment operator and it is going to increase the chosen integer by one. For example, you would use it like X++ and you would get X to be one higher than usual.
- (--)- this is the decrement operator and it is going to decrease the value of the integer by 1.

In addition to being able to use any of these that you would like, keep in mind that you are not stuck with just one of these operators in a statement. You are able to use more than one, such as a subtraction and a multiplication, in the same statement and you can use as many or as few of each one as you would like. Just remember that the program is not going to read through this from left to right, it is going to use a system that is like the order of operations so keep this in mind when you are writing out the code.

Using the comparison operators

The next type of operator that you can use is the comparison operator. These are good to use whenever you would like to put together a variable and a value inside of your statement. There are a few signs that you can use to make sure that the variable and the value are being assigned together the right way. Some of the operators that you are able to use in order to make some comparisons within JavaScript include:

- (==)—this is the equal operator and it is used to see if the value of two separate operands is equal or not. If the values are equal, your condition is going to be true.
- (!=)—this is the not equal operator and it is going to be used to check out two operands and to see if they are equal or not. If the values are not equal, the condition is going to be true.
- (>)—this is the greater than symbol. This type of operator is going to be used to see if the value of the left operand is larger than the one of the right operand. If the one on the left is greater, then the condition is true.
- (<)—this is the less than operator and it is going to be used to see if the operand on the lefthand side is lower than the operand on the righthand side. If the left hand side is less than, the condition is true.
- (>=)—this is the greater than or equal to operator. It is used to see if the value of the operand on the lefthand side is equal or greater than the value of the operand on the right side. If this is correct, the condition is going to be true.
- (<=)—this is the less than/equal to operator. This operator will be used to see if the operand on the left is equal to or less than the value of the operand on the right. If this is correct, the condition will be true.

Another thing to keep in mind with the comparison operator is that if the statement ends up being false for any of the operators that are inside the statement, the whole statement is going to be false. This is true even if nine of the operators are true but the last one is false. You could make some changes to ensure that the program acts in a certain way even if the statement ends up being false.

Using the relational operators

Relational operators make it easier to show the relationship that is going to happen between the variables and the values that come up within your code. Some of the relational operators that you are able to use inside your code include:

- (!)—when used in JavaScript, this is the logical NOT. When you see this sign, it will mean that if your operands are non-zero, the condition is going to be false.
- (||)—when you use this operator, you are using the logical OR. This one means that if any two of the operands that you are using are non-zero, the operator is going to turn the condition into a true one.
- &&--when you see this operator, you will know that it is the AND operator. This one means that if both of the operands are non-zero, the operator is going to make this a true condition.

Using the assignment operators

Another type of operator that you are able to use is the assignment operator. If you would like to work on the code and assign a variable and a value together, you will want to use the assignment operator. You will sometimes notice that the signs that are used for the assignment operator is going to look like the ones that you are using in the arithmetic operators, but they do have slightly different meanings. They are pretty self-explanatory and you will be able to see how they are used differently based on the stuff that you are putting into the code. Some of the signs that you will need to use when using the assignment operator include:

- (=)—this is the simple assignment and it is used to assign your right side value to the operand that is on the left side.
- (+=)—this is the add and assignment operator that will add together the right operand and the eft operand and then will assign this result to the operand on the left side.
- (-=)—this is the subtract and assignment. This works kind of like the previous one. You will take the right operand and then subtract it from the left operand. The result is going to be assigned to the left operand.
- (*=)—this is the multiply and assignment where you will multiply the operand on the right with the one on the left and then assign the results to the left operand.
- (/=)—this operator will divide the operand on the left side with those on the right operand and then takes this result and assigns it to the left operand.

As you can see, there are a variety of operators that you are able to use within your code to make sure that the right things are being done by the compiler. You will be able to add and subtract things together, show a relationship between your variable and your value, and so much more. This can make it easier to tell the program what to do and how it should behave when the user executes the program.

Take some time to look through these different types of operators and learn how each of them will work. You can take some time to create a few different codes and mess around with the operators to see how it is going to change the way that the code and the statement are going to work. They are simple to use and change up and the outputs that you are going to be able to get will often change based on the conditions that you set up inside the code.

Conclusion

Working in JavaScript can be a rewarding experience. It allows you to work with a lot of different programming within a website to bring something new in and make the website unique. It is fast and really easy to learn, including English words to make it even easier than some of the older languages. While you will have to make some adjustments in order to ensure that the coding will work on the different browsers, there is just so much that you can do with the JavaScript language, especially when combining with some other coding languages.

This guidebook is going to walk you through some of the steps that you need to take in order to learn how to JavaScript. This coding language is pretty simple and by the end of this guidebook, you will be able to write out at least a few of the codes that you need to get your program up and running. Whether you are newly starting out with coding or you want to expand your knowledge and learn how to use a new coding language to help you out, JavaScript is the best option for you to try out!

Before you jump on your computer, I would like you to post an HONEST REVIEW on Amazon.com in order to improve the quality of the book.

Thank you.

www.ingramcontent.com/pod-product-compliance
Lightning Source LLC
Chambersburg PA
CBHW071253050326
40690CB00011B/2383